Nomos Universitätsschriften

Betriebswirtschaftslehre

Volume 4

Konstantin Mauriz Bottenberg

Effective Collaboration at the Top of the Firm

A Behavioral Perspective

Nomos

The **Deutsche Nationalbibliothek** lists this publication in the
Deutsche Nationalbibliografie; detailed bibliographic data
are available on the Internet at http://dnb.d-nb.de

a.t.: München, Univ., Diss., 2017

ISBN   978-3-8487-4605-7 (Print)
        978-3-8452-8771-3 (ePDF)

British Library Cataloguing-in-Publication Data
A catalogue record for this book is available from the British Library.

ISBN   978-3-8487-4605-7 (Print)
        978-3-8452-8771-3 (ePDF)

Library of Congress Cataloging-in-Publication Data
Bottenberg, Konstantin Mauriz
Effective Collaboration at the Top of the Firm
A Behavioral Perspective
Konstantin Mauriz Bottenberg
124 p.

ISBN   978-3-8487-4605-7 (Print)
        978-3-8452-8771-3 (ePDF)

D 19

1st Edition 2017
© Nomos Verlagsgesellschaft, Baden-Baden, Germany 2017. Printed and bound in
Germany.

„... und ich möchte Sie, so gut ich es kann bitten, Geduld zu haben gegen alles Ungelöste in Ihrem Herzen und zu versuchen, die Fragen selbst lieb zu haben, wie verschlossene Stuben und wie Bücher, die in einer fremden Sprache geschrieben sind. Forschen Sie jetzt nicht nach den Antworten, die Ihnen nicht gegeben werden können, weil Sie sie jetzt nicht leben könnten. Und es handelt sich darum, alles zu leben. Leben Sie jetzt die Fragen. Vielleicht leben Sie dann allmählich, ohne es zu merken, eines fernen Tages in die Antworten hinein."

(Rainer Maria Rilke)

Table of Contents

List of Figures

List of Tables

List of Abbreviations

CEO	Chief executive officer
COB	Chairman of the board
COO	Chief operating officer
CV	Curriculum vitae
GCGC	German Corporate Governance Code
GMM	Generalized method of moments
OLS	Ordinary least squares
PSF	Professional service firm
R&D	Research & development
RBSC	Roland Berger Strategy Consultants
ROA	Return on assets
SIC	Standard industrial classification
SME	Small and medium-sized enterprise
TMT	Top management team
U.S.	United States
VIF	Variance inflation factor

1 General Introduction

"Proper functioning of the supervisory body and the quality of its relations with the management are among the essential conditions enabling a business to create value over the long term." (European Parliament, 2012)

While a firm's leadership has to follow many different objectives, creating value for owners and stakeholders stands above all (Jensen, 2002). The identification and examination of mechanisms, processes, and conditions under which a firm's leadership bodies create the highest value are therefore a central part of governance and management research (Carpenter & Sanders, 2009; Daily, Dalton, & Cannella, 2003). In this context, ample research provides evidence that the board of directors, top management teams (TMTs), and their interrelations have a significant influence on the performance and general prosperity of firms (Finkelstein, Hambrick, & Cannella, 2009; Hambrick, 2007). However, in leading the firm, the board of directors and TMTs have different areas of responsibility. Independent of the specifics of a local corporate governance system, a firm's top management is usually responsible for the day-to-day business activities of a firm, sets the strategic agenda, and manages its implementation (Westphal & Fredrickson, 2001). In contrast, the board of directors has the responsibility to monitor and control the work of a firm's management on the behalf of shareholders and to provide resources to the firm (Johnson, Ellstrand, & Daily, 1996). Nevertheless, both constituencies are principally united in their goal to maximize a firm's value. Accordingly, it is of high relevance for governance and management research to examine which characteristics corporate boards, TMTs as well as their constituting individuals should have in order to be effective (Finkelstein et al., 2009; Johnson, Schnatterly, & Hill, 2013), to understand under which conditions certain governance configurations create the highest value (Forbes & Milliken, 1999), and to analyze how work relations between the board of directors and a firm's management exactly affect firm outcomes (Boyd, Haynes, & Zona, 2011; Kor, 2006).

However, for a long time, studies on the board of directors and TMTs have been based on separate streams of literature (Daily & Schwenk, 1996). Only with the advancement of research on the board of directors and TMTs, more and more attention has been given to the interrelation of these two groups with each other (Carpenter, Geletkanycz, & Sanders, 2004) as well as with stakeholders inside and outside the firm (Adams, Licht, & Sagiv, 2011; Hillman & Keim, 2001). Additionally, theoretical perspectives on the relation of the board of directors and TMTs have also altered. Traditional theories, such as agency theory, often portrayed corporate boards and TMTs as opposing constituencies (Jensen & Meckling, 1976). Their relation was considered to be shaped by diverging interests and clear role separation (Jensen, 2002; Williamson, 1985). However, more recent studies acknowledge the fact that successful leadership should not be based on conflicting relations solely but rather some form of effective collaboration between members of supervisory and management boards (Carpenter, Pollock, & Leary, 2003; Kor, 2006; Westphal, 1999) as well as between a firm's leadership and other stakeholders of the firm (Adams et al., 2011; Hillman & Keim, 2001). Effective corporate governance is therefore a balance of control and collaboration (Sundaramurthy & Lewis, 2003). Additionally, the rise of the behavioral view of the firm further turned attention to sociological and psychological factors of management and governance processes and highlighted the individual and team-related aspects of leadership (Cyert & March, 1963; Westphal, 1999).

These developments are accompanied by the trend that responsibilities and roles at the top of the firm become more and more blended (Roberts & Stiles, 1999). Traditionally, the board of directors was described as the "apex of the decision control system of organizations" (Fama & Jensen, 1983, p. 311) with a clear focus on monitoring tasks. However, today, directors are also highly involved in the strategy development and implementation processes of firms (Finkelstein & Mooney, 2003; Pugliese et al., 2009). At the same time, top managers are regularly engaged in governance and compliance issues and have to deal intensively with shareholder interests. Accordingly, strong and effective relations between members of the TMT, in particular, the CEO, and the board of directors are considered to be an essential element for effective and value-oriented leadership (Boyd et al., 2011; Roberts, 2002).

While research has started to address the complex nature of TMT, board, and stakeholder interdependencies, there are many relevant gaps in the existing literature that call for attention. This dissertation addresses several of these gaps and contributes to a more nuanced and better understanding of the interplay of boards and TMTs, their constituting individuals, and important stakeholder groups of the firm. An overview of the studies presented in this dissertation, the state-of-the-art of research, and the precise research gaps each study aims to fill, is provided in the following section. Altogether, the theoretical focus lies on an integration of cognitive and social-psychological theories into existing frameworks of corporate governance research (Forbes & Milliken, 1999; Tuggle, Sirmon, Reutzel, & Bierman, 2010; Westphal & Fredrickson, 2001). The dissertation also follows calls for more integration of micro and macro perspectives in governance research (Dalton & Dalton, 2010). Based on this integrative approach, the dissertation applies a behavioral perspective on effective collaboration at the top of the firm.

1.1 Dissertation Studies

This dissertation consists of three studies of which two present empirical results based on the analysis of quantitative data and one is a conceptual study. The two empirical studies are primarily concerned with the co-work of the board of directors and a firm's top management in setting a firm's strategy. Together, the two studies aim at advancing the understanding of the special relation of these two most important decision-making groups of the firm by addressing relevant gaps in the existing corporate governance and strategic management research. The two empirical studies apply multivariate statistical methods to examine data from large panels of stock-listed firms in Germany – taking into account individual and team-level data of top managers and directors as well as firm- and industry-level data. The conceptual study integrates different streams of literature and investigates several cases to provide an analysis of current theoretical questions as well as practical concerns regarding shareholder value, stakeholder management, and Germany's corporate governance system.

The first of the two empirical studies focuses on the board of director's role to provide advice and counsel to the CEO and the TMT – the so-called advisory function of the board. In this role, directors are expected to provide "idiosyncratic knowledge and expertise to assist in the management of the firm" (Krause, Semadeni, & Cannella, 2013, p. 1629). Although research addressed the importance of board advisory from a theoretical point of view (Johnson et al., 1996; Pugliese et al., 2009), the majority of empirical studies on directors focus on their monitoring and control function within the boardroom (McDonald, Westphal, & Graebner, 2008). Accordingly, compared to board monitoring, little is known about the antecedents of effective board advisory. Only lately, a new stream of empirical studies refocuses on the examination of factors which enable individual directors and the whole board to provide effective advice and counsel (e.g. Khanna, Jones, & Boivie, 2014; Krause et al., 2013; McDonald et al., 2008).

The dissertation study continues and advances this stream of research by analyzing the influence of advisory-related director characteristics and board structural characteristics. Out of the different board functions, the advisory function depends, in particular, on effective processes (Finkelstein & Mooney, 2003; Westphal, 1999). Effective board advisory does not primarily rely on a superior expertise of directors regarding the strategy of a firm – such expertise is more pronounced within the TMT – but on the ability to ask the right questions, to intervene or guide when needed, and to assist in decision-making processes. Accordingly, we investigate if boards are more effective if directors possess high levels of advisory process expertise gained through experiences in other advisory functions, such as management consulting.

Besides directors' process-related expertise, the structural organization of the board should also play an important role in the effectiveness of advisory processes. Delineating tasks to subgroups within a board has shown to improve the work processes and the effectiveness of the whole board (Bilimoria & Piderit, 1994; Daily, 1996; Dalton, Daily, Ellstrand, & Johnson, 1998). While boards often establish committees regarding their monitoring and control tasks (i.e. audit committee, nomination committee), relatively few boards have committees for strategy-related matters. Research on subgroups of the board has missed examining the impact of non-monitoring subgroups that are not legally required (Johnson et al., 2013). Based on prior research, we argue that an advisory-oriented committee structure should contribute to more effective advice and counsel. Examining a sample of large German firms between 2004 and 2013 the study largely finds support for the proposed hypotheses. Under consideration of relevant control variables, results show that boards with a high level of expertise with advisory processes and an advisory-oriented committee structure can provide a significant increase in board effectiveness.

The second study takes a more nuanced view on the relation of boards and TMTs. It addresses the special relationship between the CEO and the chairman of the board (Roberts & Stiles, 1999). Understanding the relation of CEOs and board chairmen is important for the study of value-oriented management. Early on, studies showed that independence of the board from a CEO is a relevant prerequisite for value-maximizing strategies (Morck, Shleifer, & Vishny, 1989). While the influence of team-based characteristics of boards and TMTs on firm outcomes has received much attention in the literature (Hambrick, 2007; Johnson et al., 2013), personal relations at the top of the firm have been less examined. Although reviews of the CEO duality literature conclude that there is no consistent direct effect of CEO duality on relevant firm outcomes (Dalton et al., 1998; Krause, Semadeni, & Cannella, 2014), research has largely neglected to examine the case of CEO non-duality when a CEO is accompanied by a chairman of the board (COB). The second study addresses this gap by analyzing how career and socio-personal differences between a CEO and a COB influence a firm's R&D investment strategy. By analyzing individual characteristics of CEOs and COBs, we address a gap in the CEO duality literature which is described as "the issue with the greatest potential to generate insight, and yet with the least amount of research attention so far devoted to it" (Krause et al., 2014, p. 265).

Referring to insights about the effects of differences and diversity in teams and dyadic work relations and psychological theories about team functioning and group dynamics (Jehn & Mannix, 2001; Kor & Sundaramurthy, 2009; Littlepage, Robison, & Reddington, 1997; Schweiger, Sandberg, & Rechner, 1989; Westphal, 1999), results of this study show that differences between CEOs and COBs are generally beneficial. However, the benefits of career and socio-personal differences are contingent on the amount of shared tenure of CEOs and COBs. While benefits of career differences seem to diminish over time, the positive effects of socio-personal differences are amplified as shared tenure increases.

The third study[1] adopts a broader perspective on the role of corporate governance constituencies and different stakeholder groups for a firm's overall value creation. In the literature as well as in practice it is highly debated whether corporations should primarily follow a shareholder or a stakeholder principle (Allen, Carletti, & Marquez, 2015; Tuschke & Luber, 2012). Against the background of this debate and international corporate governance research (Aguilera, Filatotchev, Gospel, & Jackson, 2008; Aguilera & Jackson, 2010), this study investigates the current conceptualization of Germany's broader corporate governance system. Despite the in-

---

1 The third study was written jointly by Konstantin Bottenberg, Prof. Dr. Anja Tuschke, and Prof. Dr. Miriam Flickinger. The study has been published in the *Journal of Management Inquiry* (Vol 26, Issue 2, 2017).

troduction of shareholder-oriented practices, like moderate amounts of stock option pay or more transparent accounting standards (Fiss & Zajac, 2004; Sanders & Tuschke, 2007), the German corporate governance system is still considered to be a prototype of stakeholder orientation (Jackson & Moerke, 2005; Jürgens, Naumann, & Rupp, 2000).

However, critics of stakeholder systems claim that strong obligations to stakeholder interests are a drawback for firms in international competition (Aguilera & Jackson, 2010; Jensen, 2002). On the other hand, research also shows that, if applied thoughtfully, a structurally anchored stakeholder management can also have a number of advantages (Harrison, Bosse, & Phillips, 2010; Harrison & Wicks, 2013; Hillman & Keim, 2001). Drawing on case-based analyses and prior research, this study points to selected advantages of a stakeholder-oriented system, such as the active integration of stakeholder knowledge (Fauver & Fuerst, 2006; Harrison et al., 2010), greater resilience against corporate crises (Kacperczyk, 2009; Schneper & Guillén, 2004), or a long-term view on value creation and performance (Jiao, 2010; Verbeke & Tung, 2013). Admitting inherent problems arising from stakeholder orientation as well as its unique benefits, this study outlines the potentials of a modern stakeholder value system.

In the subsequent sections, the three dissertation studies are presented, followed by a general conclusion.

2 The Impact of Directors' Advisory Expertise and Advisory-oriented Board Structures on Board Effectiveness

2.1 Introduction

Over the last decades, boards have played an increasingly active governance role (Finkelstein & Mooney, 2003; Khanna et al., 2014; Pugliese et al., 2009). Although the board's primary duty may still be the control of management activities (Baysinger & Hoskisson, 1990; Fama & Jensen, 1983), the provision of advice and counsel for the upper echelons has become more and more important (Finkelstein et al., 2009; Johnson et al., 1996; Zahra & Pearce, 1989). Through advice and counsel, directors are more closely engaged in the strategy process (Westphal, 1999) and can better evaluate and influence the reasoning and assumptions of CEOs (Boyd et al., 2011). Moreover, CEOs have to prepare strategic proposals in more detail before they can convince the board (Judge & Zeithaml, 1992). Consequently, it is argued that directors' advice and counsel helps to reduce uncertainty, enhances quality, and increases the speed of strategic decision-making in face of complexity, volatility, and high demands (Johnson et al., 1996; Krause et al., 2013; McDonald et al., 2008; Rindova, 1999).

Despite the apparent role of directors' advice and counsel to support strategic decision-making at the top, research on board effectiveness has focused almost entirely on monitoring and control. The identification of different types of director knowledge and expertise and of means by which they contribute to the effectiveness of advisory activities is still rather incomplete (Johnson et al., 2013; Kor & Sundaramurthy, 2009). Similarly, knowledge about the effects of group structures and processes on board effectiveness is still limited (Finkelstein & Mooney, 2003; Forbes & Milliken, 1999; Johnson et al., 2013). We address these wide gaps from two different angles, following calls for more integrated and multilevel analyses in board research (Hillman, Shropshire, Certo, Dalton, & Dalton, 2010; Johnson et al., 2013).

First, relying on psychological theories of knowledge and expertise, we analyze in how far directors' advisory process expertise and management expertise are determinants of board effectiveness. We argue that both types of expertise reflect the ability to provide advice and counsel and expect that board effectiveness will be enhanced in general and beyond specific contexts when directors have such expertise. With respect to advisory process expertise, we suggest that experience in a professional service firm provides the ideal learning context. Professional service firms, such as management consultancies, offer knowledge-based advisory services to other organizations and are hired when organizations want to improve, change, or expand their business (Empson, Muzio, & Broschak, 2015). Employees in such firms are trained in effective service processes (Greenwood, Li, Prakash, & Deephouse, 2005; Klarner, Sarstedt, Hoeck, & Ringle, 2013), the establishment of positive client relations (Glückler & Armbrüster, 2003; Hitt, Biermant, Shimizu, & Kochhar, 2001), and in providing valuable advice in changing situations (Anand, Gardner, & Morris, 2007). In turn, directors with experience in a professional service firm should improve a board's ability to provide effective advice and counsel. Further, we acknowledge that management expertise in the boardroom is one of the most valuable sources for effective advice and counsel (Hillman, Cannella, & Paetzold, 2000; Kroll, Walters, & Le, 2007) and integrate it in our theoretical framework.

Second, we turn our attention to structural characteristics of the board that have received little attention so far. Based on theories of effective team functioning and findings about effective team processes (i.e. He & Huang, 2011; Williams & O'Reilly, 1998), we argue that boards profit from the formation of advisory-oriented subgroups. Usually, when a problem is complex and time is limited, transferring tasks to subgroups has been shown to increase the overall effectiveness of a team (Dalton et al., 1998). In boards, the most visible and prevalent type of subgroups are board committees (Adams, Hermalin, & Weisbach, 2010). Accordingly, a board's effectiveness should profit from a committee structure that is advisory-oriented. We suggest that a high advice and counsel orientation and respective effectiveness can be achieved if boards expand the number of committees to deal with tasks that go beyond the mere monitoring and control of a firm. Thus, establishing committees that focus on a firm's core business activities (e.g., technology or innovation committees) or its overall strategy (e.g., strategy committees) will help to formalize the advice and counsel role of directors and increase board effectiveness.

Our study makes several contributions to extant research. First, we go beyond prior research by examining director characteristics and structural characteristics of boards that increase board effectiveness through enhanced advice and counsel processes. We highlight the role of directors' process-related expertise and advisory-oriented board structures and contribute to both, research on board effectiveness in general and the advice and counsel role of boards in particular. Second, we offer insights for the emerging research on director expertise (Kor & Sundaramurthy, 2009; Krause et al., 2013; McDonald et al., 2008) as well as for the small body of literature on board committees (Bilimoria & Piderit, 1994; Gore, Matsunaga, & Eric Yeung, 2011; Kesner, 1988) by showing that the influence of directors' expertise on advice-giving and counsel depends on whether such expertise is more content-related and declarative or more procedural. In line with that, we provide one of the first analyses of the effects of business and strategy-related committees on firm performance. Third, by discussing and testing general indicators of board effectiveness, we aim at developing a more general framework of the advice and counsel role of boards. To the best of our knowledge, the effects of advisory process expertise and advisory-oriented board structures have not been addressed before in any work on board effectiveness. Consequently, as prior studies have not investigated these vital aspects systematically, our study contributes to a better understanding of board effectiveness and the prerequisites to successfully executing advice and counsel.

2.2 Theory and Hypotheses

2.2.1 Process-related Expertise

The expertise of directors is based on prior experiences which form and define the individual way of thinking, available knowledge repertoires, and perceptions of the environment (Hambrick & Mason, 1984; Kor & Sundaramurthy, 2009; Ployhart & Moliterno, 2011). The use of analogical reasoning allows experts to evaluate and solve problems related to their area of expertise more efficiently (Novick, 1988). Usually, experts are better able to cope with problems of information overload and time restrictions because their knowledge is more readily available and better organized (Sternberg, 1997). Therefore, experts are supposed to show "consistently superior performance on a specified set of representative tasks" (Ericsson & Charness, 1994, p. 731). Hence, expertise is essential for directors because it enables them to enact superior problem-solving and decision-making skills (Carpenter & Westphal, 2001; Hillman & Dalziel, 2003).

Indeed, some recent studies draw upon the idea that advice and counsel is more effective when directors possess high levels of expertise. McDonald et al. (2008), for instance, provide a systematic analysis of the effects of director expertise with acquisitions. Relying on a psychological model, they show that past experiences of directors with acquisitions made at other firms can positively impact the performance of a focal firm's acquisitions. In addition, a director's experience as CEO of an acquiring firm has been shown to improve the focal firm's corporate acquisition performance (Kroll, Walters, & Wright, 2008). Likewise, finance experience on the board leads to a higher inclination for acquisitions and diversification (Jensen & Zajac, 2004). Moreover, directors' international experience affects a firm's degree of internationalization (Carpenter, Sanders, & Gregersen, 2001) and choice of markets (Tuschke, Sanders, & Hernandez, 2014).

However, most individuals can only be experts in some and often rather specific domains (Ericsson & Charness, 1994). Thus, board expertise often encompasses a limited number of fields. McDonald et al. (2008) point out that expertise is often limited to issues directors have already faced in their prior work. Moreover, specific expertise of individuals and groups is highly contextual. For instance, Krause et al. (2013) show that external chief operating officers (COOs) on the board can positively impact firm performance when operational efficiency has been declining. However, under opposite conditions, they observe negative effects of COO expertise. Accordingly, one can assume that the effects of skills and competencies in the boardroom depend on a firm's current contextual situation. When firm or industry environments change, the need for certain expertise or competencies at the top of the firm also changes (Castanias & Helfat, 2001).

However, a firm's top management is usually confronted with a broad range of strategic matters that change over time and increase the demands for directors' advice and counsel (Finkelstein et al., 2009). Boards need to be able to advise management on a wide variety of aspects of a firm's strategy (Hillman & Dalziel, 2003; Westphal, 1999). Therefore, well-functioning advisory processes seem to be essential. Westphal (1999) shows, for instance, that firm performance is positively influenced by the perceived quality and intensity of collaboration between directors and the CEO. Further, Carpenter and Westphal (2001) find that a successful involvement of directors in strategic decision-making does not depend on the mere amount of knowledge directors bring to the boardroom but more on the fit of their knowledge with the business environment of a firm.

While a firm's top management team is responsible for developing and implementing the strategy, directors influence strategic decisions indirectly through monitoring, advice, and counsel (Boyd et al., 2011). In the light of an indirect involvement of directors in strategic decisions, the effectiveness of advisory interactions between directors and the top management team seems crucial. Directors need to possess skills and knowledge not only regarding specific strategic matters at hand but also regarding an effective provision of advice and counsel. Therefore, it is important for boards to have expertise related to the general advisory process. Such expertise will contribute to board effectiveness independent of specific strategic decisions or contextual conditions.

2.2.2 Advisory Process Expertise

Knowledge theorists distinguish between declarative and procedural knowledge (Argote & Miron-Spektor, 2011). Declarative knowledge can be articulated and codified, easily transferred, and is learned through formal education (Liebeskind, 1996; Nonaka & von Krogh, 2009). In contrast, procedural or tacit knowledge is difficult to articulate and to transmit between individuals. Thus, it can only be acquired through experience (Berman, Down, & Hill, 2002; Kogut & Zander, 1993; Teece, Pisano, & Shuen, 1997). Knowledge about how to advise others effectively is mainly tacit and procedural and can, therefore, almost only be gained from prior experience in functions which entail professional advisory activities. Consequently, it can be argued that directors are best able to provide effective advice and counsel for the firm's top management if they possess experience in roles in which they have acquired procedural knowledge about respective advisory processes. We assume that work experience in a professional service firm (PSF) provides the opportunity to develop such expertise. PSFs are defined as companies with highly educated employees and intangible outputs based on complex knowledge which makes them distinct from other firms in several ways (Greenwood et al., 2005).

Employees of PSFs typically exhibit above average skills and competencies and can substantially increase their knowledge while progressing in their career (Empson et al., 2015; Hitt et al., 2001). As directors are confronted with highly complex tasks (Forbes & Milliken, 1999), and accumulation of explicit knowledge is restricted by limited information processing capabilities (Khanna et al., 2014), those trained in knowledge intensive PSFs should be a major source of effective advice and counsel.

Trained and socialized in professional service roles (Fosstenløkken, Løwendahl, & Revang, 2003), those directors will likely have a high motivation to deliver excellent service. This also influences the board as a whole because individual efforts influence overall expectations about fulfilling certain tasks (Forbes & Milliken, 1999). Thus, strong effort norms of PSF-experienced directors can improve the board's effectiveness in advising and counseling management as all directors will spend more time and diligence towards advisory-related duties.

Furthermore, structures and resources in PSFs are particularly designed to generate and deliver new knowledge as employees develop systematic approaches to integrate existing knowledge into client-specific projects (Haas & Hansen, 2005; Werr & Stjernberg, 2003). In the dynamic, project-based work of PSFs, members of project teams need to be able to tap into the knowledge of their colleagues and combine it with their own knowledge to perform their tasks effectively (Gardner, Gino, & Staats, 2012). PSFs have to respond quickly to the changing needs of their clients and, accordingly, try to renew their knowledge structures constantly (Anand et al., 2007; Hitt, Bierman, Uhlenbruck, & Shimizu, 2006). Thus, directors with experience in a PSF are highly trained in how to use and combine existing knowledge to satisfy the needs of a service recipient. Likewise, they are trained to communicate effectively which researchers also stressed to be critical for the relationship between directors and TMT members (Finkelstein & Mooney, 2003; Westphal, 1999).

In total, main features of the advisory role of directors are similar to those of employees in PSFs. Taken together, as knowledge transfer is enhanced when situations or problems show similar structural relations (Gary, Wood, & Pillinger, 2012), we propose the baseline hypothesis that *board effectiveness is positively associated with the proportion of directors' with experience from working in a PSF.*

As we outlined above, directors with PSF experience likely contribute to board effectiveness because of their procedural knowledge on how to provide effective advice and counsel. While the specific expertise of directors may differ depending on the PSF they worked for, all service-oriented firms are likely to foster directors' ability to provide advice and counsel for management. However, we take into account that directors' ability to fulfill their advisory role may to some extent vary depending on whether they worked for a PSF specialized in management consulting or for those that offer law or accounting-related services. While management consulting is often future-oriented and directed towards developing new strategies (Anand et al., 2007), law and accounting-related services are often more concerned with issues that occurred in the firm's immediate past. In addition, management consulting is by and large focused on the focal firm's success in the market whereas law and accounting-related services mostly provide administrative support (Empson et al., 2015; von Nordenflycht, 2010). To capture the potential differences of PSF experience in more business-oriented PSFs (management consulting) compared to more support-oriented PSFs (law and accounting), we propose the following two separate hypotheses:

Hypothesis 1 a: The proportion of a focal firm's directors with advisory process expertise – from a management consulting firm – is positively related to board effectiveness.

Hypothesis 1 b: The proportion of a focal firm's directors with advisory process expertise – from a law or accounting firm – is positively related to board effectiveness.

2.2.3 Management Expertise

Besides advisory process expertise gained from previous work in PSFs, we also consider the experience of directors gained in top management positions. Not surprisingly, research shows that firms have a preference for directors with such expertise because they are deemed to be best suited for providing advice to top managers (Finkelstein et al., 2009; Kroll et al., 2007). In contrast to directors without respective management expertise who often suffer from a lack of knowledge regarding the day-to-day activities of TMT members, management experts can act as a "sounding board" based on their broader knowledge about strategic and managerial concerns (Hillman et al., 2000). Additionally, management experts may be able to provide knowledge that the TMT is currently lacking (Kroll et al., 2007). It is also assumed that "individual member expertise is most beneficial to the extent that high-expertise members have relatively high levels of influence" (McDonald et al., 2008, p. 1172). Accordingly, the authority of management experts, such as "director-CEOs", can leverage the influence of their advice.

However, research shows that it is very difficult to effectively transfer knowledge from one setting to another because individuals often struggle with identifying structurally similar situations in which they can apply prior knowledge (Gary et al., 2012). Moreover, individuals find it problematic to evaluate the performance of others if they do not have high levels of experience with similar tasks (Bandura, 1997). Accordingly, the more similar a director's management experience to the setting in which it is applied, the more smoothly it can be transferred.

Nevertheless, many studies rely on rather broad conceptualizations of management expertise, such as any business-related expertise, disregarding which specific aspects are relevant and more likely transferred (Hillman et al., 2000; Johnson et al., 2013). To capture the aspects of directors' management expertise helping to improve advisory processes in boardrooms more specifically, we focus on up-to-date expertise gained in TMT positions in similar firm settings. We believe that directors who are current top managers of another firm can better understand the needs of the focal firm's TMT members. This includes, for instance, knowing when a TMT member most likely needs advice, understanding time constraints and other pressures of executives, and integrating this knowledge into the advice and counsel process.

With this narrow conceptualization of management expertise, we depart from prior studies assuming that any business-related expertise will enable directors to advise the CEO or other members of the TMT effectively (Hillman et al., 2000). In addition, the rarity of an experience is an important and valuable characteristic which has received much attention in recent organizational research (Argote & Miron-Spektor, 2011). With respect to boardroom discussions, we expect no scarcity of general expertise with business-related issues or with the focal firm's industry. In contrast, current and qualified top management expertise is likely to be scarce (Krause et al., 2013). Thus, we hypothesize:

Hypothesis 2:   *The proportion of a focal firm's directors with management expertise from a current top management position in another firm is positively related to board effectiveness.*

2.2.4 Advisory-oriented Board Structures

With respect to the relation between directors and members of the top management team, board processes are typically highly complex due to limited time spans, incomplete information, and multifaceted relationships. Consequently, effective advice-giving for the focal firm's TMT depends not only on an individual or team-based expertise but, moreover, on the ability of directors to interact and communicate effectively. Against this background, it has been argued that structural characteristics are an important factor for increasing effectiveness (Dalton et al., 1998) and that the formation of stable subgroups (i.e., board committees) helps boards to achieve higher efficiency (Bilimoria & Piderit, 1994; Kesner, 1988). Accordingly, the formation of committees which meet separately and have responsibility for defined tasks has become a common standard for larger boards. Critical board decisions are prepared in those committees before they are discussed by the board as a whole (Daily, 1996). Thus, critical information-processing and opinion-forming take place in board committees.

In general, there are two basic mechanisms of group work and group decision-making that explain why the formation of smaller subgroups can increase the effectiveness of boards. First, coordination and communication are easier and more effective in smaller groups (Goodstein, Gautam, & Boeker, 1994; Gore et al., 2011). This also helps to guide broader boardroom interactions. Second, knowledge and expertise is more concentrated in board committees and focused towards a particular topic. High levels of expertise in a group typically lead to better decisions (McDonald et al., 2008) and the focus on specific issues reduces role ambiguity and task complexity (Finkelstein & Mooney, 2003; He & Huang, 2011; Lorsch & MacIver, 1989).

However, in a recent review of board research, Johnson et al. (2013) note that research on subgroups has missed examining in how far board committees – beyond those legally required – impact strategy and performance. While researchers noted early on that a board's strategy-related tasks could profit from the formation of respective committees (Harrison, 1987; Henke, 1986), the influence of committee structures on board functions beyond monitoring has rarely been examined (Kaczmarek, Kimino, & Pye, 2012). Bearing in mind that board advice and counsel is mainly concerned with the future strategic positioning of a firm, it is different from the monitoring role which is more oriented towards the current status, approval of existing plans, or compliance issues. To improve advice and counsel, boards cannot rely on formal structures that are established primarily to enhance the monitoring function. Rather, to add to the effectiveness of boards, the establishment of committees directed at the general business and strategy of a firm seems to be helpful.

We expect that committees on business-related issues lead to better advice and counsel for several reasons. First, the above-mentioned benefits of smaller groups, such as improved coordination and communication, are also essential for advisory processes (Forbes & Milliken, 1999). Closer work relations in smaller groups enable the use of more unique knowledge and facilitate coordination as well as sharing of know-how (Williams & O'Reilly, 1998) which in turn can impact the effectiveness of directors' advice and counsel (Tian, Haleblian, & Rajagopalan, 2011). Common language and shared understandings make it easier to communicate (Grant, 1996) and are likely increased when directors prepare business-related decisions in smaller groups. This helps to overcome communication barriers often present in larger boards (Goodstein et al., 1994).

Second, many argue that board effectiveness is hindered by time constraints affecting especially those directors who are commonly viewed as having the greatest expertise to provide excellent advice, such as CEOs of other firms or experienced directors with multiple board memberships (Westphal, 1999). Effective advice and counsel requires in-depth reasoning and sufficient discussions which can be time-consuming. In practice, boards "are often hard pressed to get beyond compliance-related topics to secure the breathing space needed for developing strategy" (Bhagat, Hirt, & Kehoe, 2013, p. 2). Moreover, research on the attention-based view of the firm (Tuggle et al., 2010) notes that the allocation of attention of board members to their many responsibilities is highly influenced by the way they interact. Accordingly, if many different functional aspects of board work compete for the limited time and attention of directors (Hillman & Dalziel, 2003; Tuggle et al., 2010), the presence of business-related committees will help to turn director attention to strategy and related advisory issues.

Third, advisory-oriented committee structures may help to overcome problems of pluralistic ignorance that commonly occur in board discussion on strategy (Westphal & Bednar, 2005). Pluralistic ignorance as "the failure of directors to express their concerns about corporate strategy" (Westphal & Bednar, 2005, p. 268), is a common impairment of decision-making in corporate boards. Specialized committees that put the discussion of issues related to a firm's business on their agenda can reduce this problem because it is easier for directors to raise concerns about existing plans and practices during committee meetings. Accordingly, we hypothesize:

Hypothesis 3 a: The existence of board committees that are concerned with specific areas of a firm's business activities is positively related to board effectiveness.

We further consider the impact of committees that are not focused on a specific business area of the focal firm but more generally on strategic matters. Those strategy committees can provide a board with the ability to react timely to emergent and more general strategic challenges (Harrison, 1987). The discussion and evaluation of a firm's overall strategy within those committees help directors to fulfill their role as a strategic partner of the top management team in a more systematic way (Rindova, 1999). A committee dealing with a firm's general strategy could thus further contribute to the effectiveness of board advice and counsel. Moreover, having such a committee reflects the intention to deal intensively with the future direction of a firm and to engage actively in discussions about strategy. As board involvement in strategy has shown to increase firm performance (Judge & Zeithaml, 1992), strategy committees should be positively related to performance outcomes. Therefore, we propose:

Hypothesis 3 b: The existence of board committees that are concerned with a firm's general strategy is positively related to board effectiveness.

2.3 Methods

2.3.1 Sample and Data

We use a panel data set to test our hypotheses empirically. Our sample is based on an index consisting of the 110 largest stock-listed firms in Germany (HDAX). The HDAX represents almost the entire market capitalization of the German stock market and includes a broad range of firms from many different industries which vary in their size and age. To observe effects over time, our sample covers a ten-year period, ranging from 2004 to 2013. Firms were included in the sample if they had been listed in the HDAX for more than three consecutive years within this time frame. Due to bankruptcy, acquisition, or delisting, some firms were dropped. Similar samples have been used in other empirical studies of German firms (e.g. Fiss & Zajac, 2004; Sanders & Tuschke, 2007).

Data on director characteristics were collected from various sources such as corporate websites, databases on executive backgrounds (e.g. *Bloomberg executive profiles*, *Munzinger Online*), or annual reports. To assess a director's career background and his or her track of professional experience we analyzed the respective curriculum vitae (CV) and extracted all career-related information. Likewise, we collected information on the committee structure of firms and evaluated the description of tasks and activities of board committees available from a firm's annual report and other company statements. In total, we analyzed several hundred descriptions of board committees and examined a couple of thousand director CVs. Data on the firm-level were gathered from the *Worldscope* database as well as annual reports.

We note that Germany as the empirical context of our study has some important characteristics that may influence the role of board advice and counsel. A unique characteristic of Germany's corporate governance is the clear separation of management and supervisory functions. Members of the supervisory board are not allowed to serve on the management board of the same firm and vice versa. In the German two-tier system, the management board is responsible for all firm operations while the supervisory board is focused on monitoring management and providing advice. A further characteristic of German boards is employee co-determination. Depending on the size of the firm, one-third or even one-half of all seats on a supervisory board can be assigned to employee representatives.

2.3.2 Variables

Dependent variable. Boards usually pay high attention to the performance of a firm because it is their primary duty to secure value creation and profit maximization in the interest of shareholders (Fama & Jensen, 1983). Especially because of the reputational consequences for themselves as board members of high or poorly performing firms (Tuggle et al., 2010). Accordingly, the board literature assumes that the overall board effectiveness is best measured by indicators of firm performance (Dalton et al., 1998; Deutsch, 2005). Moreover, board participation in strategic decisions has been linked to firm performance before (e.g. Judge & Zeithaml, 1992; Westphal, 1999). Therefore, and in line with prior literature, we rely on an indicator of firm performance to assess the effectiveness of board advice and counsel.

We operationalized board effectiveness using *Tobin's Q*. In the context of our study, Tobin's Q is a very powerful and relevant indicator of performance and board effectiveness as it reflects the market perceptions about the future value of a firm's strategic position. In comparison to accounting-based performance measures, such as return on assets (ROA) or return on sales, Tobin's Q has the advantage of reflecting the overall value of a firm rather than a sum of its parts. Following commonly used definitions, we measure Tobin's Q as the ratio of the market value of a firm to the book value of a firm's total assets with market value computed as the sum of the market year end value of a firm's common and outstanding shares, the book value of a firm's long-term debts, and the book value of a firm's current, short-term liabilities (Brush, Bromiley, & Hendrickx, 2000; Kim & Bettis, 2014). Short-term liabilities are all debts or obligations of a firm that have to be satisfied within one year. Tobin's Q is a forward-looking measure of firm performance, while ROA and similar measures are backward-looking. Moreover, Tobin's Q is less affected by the influence of different tax rates, laws, or accounting procedures (Wernerfelt & Montgomery, 1988). In the context of board effectiveness, it is also worth to note that investors of a firm, which ultimately define the level of Tobin's Q, also pay more and more attention to the work and composition of the board (Kroll et al., 2007; Tian et al., 2011). Therefore, the level of Tobin's Q is likely to reflect the effectiveness of a board better than many other measures of firm performance.

Independent variables. We defined directors' *advisory process expertise* as prior work experience in a PSF. In line with the literature, we focused on the most common types of PSFs, i.e., consultancies, accounting firms, and law firms (von Nordenflycht, 2010). To identify if directors have worked in such companies, we analyzed their career over time based on their CVs. To verify firms as PSFs, we cross-checked lists of PSFs available from related professional associations. In addition, we analyzed the information provided by the firms' corporate website, if available. Only if a firm could be validated as PSF through these cross-checks, we counted the particular experience for the directors in question. Further, we distinguish between prior work experience with consulting (*advisory process expertise from management consulting*) from experience in law or accounting firms (*advisory process expertise from law and accounting*).

Directors have *management expertise* if they are currently CEO or a TMT member in another firm (Kroll et al., 2007). To ensure that our measure is capturing the process aspects of management expertise we are interested in, we only consider CEO or TMT experience in other HDAX firms. Moreover, we only count experience gained in current positions to make sure that the respective expertise is not outdated. Following prior studies (Tian et al., 2011; Westphal & Zajac, 1997), we created board-level measures for all three director expertise variables by dividing the number of directors with advisory process or management expertise by board size measured as the total number of directors serving on a focal firm's board.

We also assume that the committee structure of a board is more advisory-oriented when it includes committees which are not purely focused on monitoring issues (e.g., audit committee) or personnel-related control activities (e.g., nomination committee, compensation committee) but are concerned with a firm's business activities. While the establishment of monitoring and personnel-related committees is predetermined by law and corporate governance standards[2], the formation of additional committees is optional. Accordingly, the variable *business committees* measures if boards have established committees which have a non-monitoring, non-personnel focus but are directed towards a firm's primary business activities.

We argued that beyond the effects of business committees, the presence of committees which are clearly focused on a firm's strategy foster an effective advisory process. We measured the presence of *strategy committees* by evaluating whether a committee is explicitly labeled as *strategy* or *strategic* committee or explicitly described as focusing on *general* firm strategy. To assess the focus of committees we analyzed the description of each committee of every sample firm in each year within our time frame.

Control variables. Our dependent variable Tobin's Q can be influenced by a number of industry-, firm-, and board-related factors. For instance, industries can vary with regard to their potential to create firm value. Therefore, we included two industry-related control measures. First, we controlled for *industry growth*. Whether an industry is growing or not is

---

2 In the U.S., the Sarbanes-Oxley Act requires to build an audit, a compensation, and a nomination committee (Dalton & Dalton, 2010). In Germany, the German Corporate Governance Code (GCGC) suggests to build at least an audit and a nomination committee.

likely to affect shareholder expectations about firm value which influences Tobin's Q. To measure industry growth, firms were categorized based on their four-digit standard industrial classification (SIC) code. For each four-digit SIC code, we computed the three-year growth rate of sales. Additionally, we controlled for industry performance. For each year in our sample, the average Tobin's Q of all firms operating in the same industry was calculated to measure *average industry performance*. To avoid problems with multicollinearity, we used SIC codes at the one-digit level. More nuanced levels of SIC codes caused very high correlations of average industry performance with general firm performance.

At the firm-level, we controlled for *firm size*, measured as the number of total employees, and for *firm age*, measured as years since foundation. Further, we included two firm-specific variables that can be associated with the level of Tobin's Q. First, we controlled for a firm's debt structure by including the *leverage* of a firm, measured as debt over assets (Walls, Berrone, & Phan, 2012). Likewise, the level of a firm's capital expenditures can be a major influencing factor in our context. In fact, Tobin's Q can, for instance, be affected by underinvestment. Therefore, we also controlled for a firm's *capital intensity*, measured as the ratio of capital expenditures to sales. We also controlled for variables that may systematically influence investor perceptions about a firm and in turn influence Tobin's Q. We controlled for *market capitalization* and whether a firm in our sample is a *DAX member*. The DAX is an index capturing the 30 largest stock-listed firms in Germany and is comparable to the Dow Jones Industrial Average for firms listed in the United States. Companies in the DAX have a much higher visibility to investors.

Regarding the board level, we controlled for the *number of director board ties*. Director board ties can influence board effectiveness and firm outcomes (Johnson et al., 2013). Directors with additional appointments in other boards profit from their exposure to many different business contexts and strategic issues (Carpenter & Westphal, 2001). However, multiple board appointments have also been linked to problems, such as time constraints or limited information processing demands (Khanna et al., 2014). Accordingly, multiple board appointments can also reduce the ability to engage in effective board advice and counsel activities. Further, CEO duality and the percentage of outside directors are often used in studies on board effectiveness (He & Huang, 2011). However, these two measures are not included in our set of control variables because the German governance system does not allow for CEO duality and does permit directors to be part of a firm's management team. Accordingly, our empirical setting naturally controls for these two important factors. Lastly, for the ten-year period under study, we included nine *year* dummy variables to control for time effects. Year dummy variables are not displayed in the regression table but were included in all models.

2.3.3 Data Analysis

We are interested in how far director expertise and board committees influence board effectiveness measured as Tobin's Q. However, board composition and director decisions are not exogenously determined but influenced by firm characteristics or prior choices (Johnson et al., 2013). For instance, if directors possess high amounts of human capital they are often in a position to choose between different potential directorships and, in turn, can decide to serve in firms with higher performance levels (Boivie, Graffin, & Pollock, 2012). Not only can the composition of a board be influenced by firm outcomes but also the behavior of board members. For instance, board involvement can be affected by different performance levels (Westphal & Fredrickson, 2001). Moreover, the prior performance of a firm has been shown, for instance, to influence the advice-seeking behavior of CEOs (McDonald & Westphal, 2003). Taking these results into account, our empirical analysis could be clouded by endogeneity problems. Researchers have stressed the issue of endogeneity in empirical research on boards (Tuschke et al., 2014) or top management teams (Dezsö & Ross, 2012). While we have a substantial theoretical rational to assume that board characteristics influence firm performance, we are also aware of the fact that endogeneity is likely to be a severe threat to our argumentation.

We followed a widely accepted approach to control for endogeneity problems applying a dynamic panel data model with the use of an Arellano-Bond estimator (Arellano & Bond, 1991). The Arellano-Bond estimator is based on the generalized method of moments (GMM) technique. It is designed specifically for panels like ours with shorter time frames and a larger number of firms. To account for the fact that the presence of directors with advisory or management process expertise and the establishment of advisory-oriented board structures might be influenced by previous performance levels, we controlled for prior firm performance. However, including the lagged dependent variable in a regression analysis can lead to autocorrelation with error terms (Greene, 2000). The dynamic panel approach of Arellano-Bond addresses this problem by first-differencing and then instrumenting the lagged dependent variable by appropriate higher lagged levels. The use of first differences also eliminates firm fixed-effects. This also includes unobserved firm-fixed effects and thus helps to reduce potential endogeneity concerns regarding unobserved variables. A further advantage of the GMM technique is that a normal distribution of residuals is not required. GMM produces consistent estimates which are asymptotically normal, even when the dependent variable has a non-normal distribution (Hansen, 1982). Therefore, problems of skewness or censoring of Tobin's Q are eased as well as potential problems of serial correlation or heteroscedasticity of residuals (Arellano & Bond, 1991).

We are further aware that the results of multivariate regression analysis can be affected by outliers – especially if they are present within the distribution of the dependent variable (Rousseeuw & Leroy, 2005). To ensure that our analysis is not vulnerable to this threat, we winsorized our dependent variable at the 1st and 99th percentile of the distribution (David, O'Brien, Yoshikawa, & Delios, 2010).

2.4 Results

Table 1 shows descriptive statistics and correlations for all variables. Correlations between variables in our study were moderate, except correlations between market capitalization and firm size and market capitalization and being a DAX member. High correlations between these variables are expected because larger firms usually have a higher market capitalization and the DAX index comprises the largest stock-listed firms in Germany. Nevertheless, to test whether our models are biased by multicollinearity, we computed an ordinary least squares (OLS) regression to calculate variance inflation factors (VIFs). Results show that all VIFs are well below the critical value of 10 (Kutner, Nachtsheim, & Neter, 2004) with the highest VIF for a single variable being 4.01 and the average VIF for all variables being 2.04.

Table 2 presents the results of the Arellano-Bond analysis. Model 1 shows the results for the control variables. Model 2 is showing the effect of our baseline hypothesis regarding PSF experienced directors. Further, Models 3 to 5 show the results with regard to the hypothesized effects of advisory process expertise, management expertise and committee structure in a hierarchical manner. Model 6 is the full model including all independent variables. Robust standard errors are reported in parentheses for all coefficients.

Arellano and Bond (1991) suggest applying different specification tests to assess the validity of dynamic panel data models. For each model, these specification tests are reported at the end of the table. Following their suggestions, we tested whether our results were harmed by unwanted autocorrelations between residuals in first or second differences and if instruments were valid. By construction, residuals should be correlated in first differences (AR(1)) but should not be correlated in second differences (AR(2)). Significance for the AR(1) test statistic means that residuals in first differences are correlated. Lack of significance for the AR(2) test statistic means that there is no serial correlation in second differences. Lack of significance for the Hansen test statistic means that overidentification restrictions are valid. Results show that first- and second-order autocorrelations are as intended, indicating the correct specification of moment conditions. The Hansen test statistic reports that models are not affected by overidentification. Additionally, test statistics for the Wald Chi-Square test are significant ($p < 0.001$) in all models.

The baseline hypothesis that PSF experience of directors positively influences board effectiveness, measured as Tobin's Q, is confirmed. The effect of advisory process expertise (from any PSF type) is positive and significant ($\beta = 1.316$, $p < 0.01$). The first two hypotheses more precisely predicted that the proportion of directors with advisory process expertise from management consulting firms (H1 a) and law and accounting firms (H1 b) positively influences board effectiveness. Model 3 shows that these hypotheses are supported. Both, advisory process expertise from management consulting firms ($\beta = 1.109$, $p < 0.05$) and from accounting and law firms ($\beta = 1.498$, $p < 0.05$) positively impact Tobin's Q. Model 4 shows that the single effect of management expertise is positive but not significant. In the full model, the effect of management expertise is positive and significant ($\beta = 1.245$, $p < 0.10$).

Hypothesis 3 a suggested that the presence of committees concerned with a firm's business activities contributes to the effectiveness of boards. The results also support this hypothesis as the effect of business committees on Tobin's Q is positive and significant ($\beta = 0.199$, $p < 0.01$). However, regarding hypothesis 3 b, the influence of strategy committees, the effect is not significant ($\beta = 0.089$, $p > 0.10$).

Table 1: Descriptive Statistics and Correlations (Study 1)

Variable	Mean	SD	1	2	3	4	5	6	7	8	9	10	11	12	13	14	15
1 Firm performance	1.52	1.12															
2 Industry average performance	1.52	0.48	0.42														
3 Industry growth	11.52	37.75	0.05	0.06													
4 Firm size[a]	9.33	2.02	-0.30	0.14	-0.18												
5 Firm age[a]	3.79	1.08	-0.17	-0.10	-0.15	0.38											
6 Leverage[a]	2.69	1.31	-0.34	-0.16	-0.06	0.21	0.06										
7 Capital intensity[a]	1.41	0.99	-0.10	-0.22	-0.13	0.02	-0.07	0.29									
8 DAX member	0.28	0.45	-0.15	-0.06	-0.05	0.60	0.14	0.13	0.15								
9 Market capitalization[a]	7.88	1.59	-0.06	0.04	-0.11	0.74	0.28	0.12	0.21	0.75							
10 Number of director board ties	1.94	2.05	-0.28	-0.04	-0.08	0.62	0.21	0.17	0.18	0.66	0.62						
11 Advisory process expertise (all)	0.09	0.11	0.20	-0.05	-0.05	-0.27	-0.27	0.02	0.02	-0.00	-0.13	-0.07					
12 Advisory process expertise (management consulting)	0.05	0.08	0.04	-0.12	-0.03	-0.30	-0.22	0.11	0.16	-0.00	-0.13	-0.00	0.70				
13 Advisory process expertise (accounting and law)	0.04	0.08	0.24	0.06	-0.04	-0.06	-0.15	-0.09	-0.14	0.00	-0.04	-0.09	0.66	-0.07			
14 Management expertise	0.04	0.06	-0.16	-0.03	-0.00	0.29	0.09	0.05	0.04	0.24	0.25	0.41	-0.02	-0.06	0.03		
15 Business committees	0.36	0.48	-0.15	-0.03	-0.08	0.32	0.10	0.21	0.03	0.20	0.23	0.23	-0.07	-0.01	-0.09	0.05	
16 Strategy committees	0.16	0.37	-0.10	-0.08	0.01	0.08	-0.08	0.01	0.00	0.06	0.04	0.07	0.09	0.04	0.08	0.13	-0.33

$N = 673$; correlations greater than $|0.03|$ are significant at $p < 0.05$. [a] Variables are log-transformed

Table 2: Arellano-Bond Analysis of Tobin's Q

Variables	Model 1	Model 2	Model 3	Model 4	Model 5	Model 6
Firm performance $_{t-1}$	0.229*	0.208*	0.208*	0.226*	0.211*	0.188*
	(0.096)	(0.098)	(0.099)	(0.095)	(0.094)	(0.094)
Industry average performance	0.620***	0.603***	0.606***	0.624***	0.601***	0.593***
	(0.135)	(0.132)	(0.132)	(0.134)	(0.131)	(0.127)
Industry growth	-0.001*	-0.001*	-0.001*	-0.001*	-0.001*	-0.001*
	(0.001)	(0.001)	(0.001)	(0.001)	(0.001)	(0.001)
Firm size	-0.618***	-0.594***	-0.593***	-0.607***	-0.599***	-0.564***
	(0.126)	(0.118)	(0.117)	(0.121)	(0.122)	(0.110)
Firm age	-0.111	-0.099	-0.108	-0.092	-0.064	-0.040
	(0.285)	(0.287)	(0.283)	(0.287)	(0.294)	(0.294)
Leverage	0.016	0.012	0.012	0.010	0.013	0.004
	(0.053)	(0.049)	(0.049)	(0.053)	(0.052)	(0.048)
Capital intensity	-0.134**	-0.122**	-0.123**	-0.141**	-0.132**	-0.127***
	(0.045)	(0.041)	(0.041)	(0.043)	(0.043)	(0.038)
DAX member	-0.255*	-0.259*	-0.259*	-0.258*	-0.248*	-0.250*
	(0.129)	(0.129)	(0.128)	(0.125)	(0.126)	(0.121)
Market capitalization	0.421***	0.449***	0.449***	0.419***	0.422***	0.445***
	(0.086)	(0.083)	(0.083)	(0.086)	(0.085)	(0.083)
Number of director board ties	0.013	0.009	0.009	0.008	0.014	0.006
	(0.019)	(0.019)	(0.019)	(0.019)	(0.019)	(0.019)
Year dummies	Y	Y	Y	Y	Y	Y
Advisory process expertise (all)		1.316**				
		(0.446)				
Advisory process expertise (management consulting)			1.109*			1.148*
			(0.463)			(0.451)
Advisory process expertise (accounting and law)			1.498*			1.386*
			(0.636)			(0.578)
Management expertise				1.284		1.245+
				(0.797)		(0.710)
Business committees					0.199**	0.170*
					(0.070)	(0.068)
Strategy committees					0.089	0.023
					(0.082)	(0.087)
Constant	3.336+	2.750	2.779	3.185	2.911	2.246
	(2.023)	(1.954)	(1.954)	(1.973)	(1.997)	(1.907)
Number of observations, firms	673, 93	673, 93	673, 93	673, 93	673, 93	673, 93
Model Chi²	272.37***	274.14***	295.29***	331.71***	371.21***	437.12***
Specification test statistics						
Serial correlation: AR(1)	-2.93**	-2.97**	-2.98**	-3.19**	-3.02**	-3.33**
Serial correlation: AR(2)	-0.13	-0.51	-0.53	-0.10	0.04	-0.31
Overidentification: Hansen	43.33	45.12	46.46+	46.08+	42.13	43.62

*** p<0.001; ** p<0.01; * p<0.05; + p<0.1. Two-tailed hypothesis tests. Robust standard errors in parentheses.

Robustness checks. To ensure that correcting for outliers did not fundamentally change results, we re-ran our analysis using an un-winsorized dependent variable. This change in the dependent variable did not alter the direction of results but slightly lowered the level of significance for management expertise and advisory process expertise. Additionally, we ran several regressions with further control variables. For instance, we included more firm-related variables such as R&D intensity and several further director characteristics such as average age or average tenure. However, model specification tests reported that those extended models were not completely fulfilling the necessary criteria of a valid dynamic panel data model. Therefore, we only included the most relevant control variables in the final models to avoid problems of overidentification.

Regarding the effects of management expertise, we also conducted a supplementary analysis in which we defined management expertise more precisely. As described above, many studies on management expertise at the board level only consider CEO experience while further top management team experience is often ignored (Krause et al., 2013). As our variable of management expertise includes CEOs as well as other TMT members, we wanted to know which of these types of expertise contributes to the effect in our main analysis. Therefore, we separated management expertise into management expertise from CEO positions and management expertise from other TMT positions. Results show that only management expertise from CEO positions has a positive and significant effect on Tobin's Q while management expertise from further TMT positions has no significant effect. Thus, supporting our theoretical rationale that the relevant contribution of management expertise to the advice and counsel role stems from the improved understanding of director-CEOs who can more easily relate to the focal firm's top management.

2.5 Discussion

The question of what makes boards effective is at the center of corporate governance research. An effective board contributes positively to a firm's strategic orientation and its overall performance. To do so, boards have to excel in multiple aspects of their work (Daily et al., 2003; Hillman & Dalziel, 2003). This includes monitoring and control of a firm's top management as well as the provision of advice and counsel to support strategic decision-making (Johnson et al., 1996). However, research on board effectiveness has largely focused on the monitoring role of boards (Daily et al., 2003) while the advice and counsel role has received considerably less attention. Accordingly, empirical research on the advisory role of boards is still in its beginning stage (McDonald et al., 2008).

To understand what drives effective advisory processes at the board, we argue that it is beneficial to consider more than one level of analysis because effective processes can be enhanced by skills of individuals within a team but also by more efficient team structures. Accordingly, we use a multilevel approach (Dalton & Dalton, 2010) and develop a theoretical model on how director expertise, micro-structures of the board, and board effectiveness are connected. In addition, we regard macro and micro perspectives in our theoretical model by linking the board literature with psychological literature on knowledge, expertise, and team processes.

We find that the presence of directors with advisory process expertise gained from work experience in a PSF positively affects board effectiveness measured as Tobin's Q. Experience in a PSF obviously provides a type of competence that can hardly be acquired in other functions or industries. Thus, the integration of directors trained in delivering professionalized advisory services can be a strategic asset for firms. Likewise, our results show that directors with management expertise are a valuable asset for firms. Knowledge about the challenges of being, for instance, a CEO is mainly tacit and therefore not easily available (Tian et al., 2011). Accordingly, knowledge structures that are indicated by knowledge about these challenges are valuable because they help a board to adapt their advice-giving to the needs of the focal firm's top management. Interestingly, Krause et al. (2013) note that the lack of studies analyzing director expertise as executives of other firms is one possible reason for the limited knowledge about the implications of director expertise for firm performance. Additionally, much of what makes up for excellent advisory service is tacit and implicit in nature (Fosstenløkken et al., 2003; Hitt et al., 2001). It is often difficult to evaluate the quality of a certain explicit advice and to judge its effect on firm performance (Carpenter & Westphal, 2001).

Our study on the process-related expertise of directors contributes to a recent stream of empirical studies focusing on the advice and counsel role of boards and its impact on overall board effectiveness. Prior literature reports, for instance, positive effects of directors acquisition expertise on corporate acquisition performance (Kroll et al., 2008; McDonald et al.,

2008), of CEO experience on evaluation of CEO appointments (Tian et al., 2011), or of COO expertise on operational efficiency (Krause et al., 2013). These studies provided important steps towards a better understanding of the advice and counsel role of boards. However, common to them is a focus on the context-related expertise of directors and special situations in which some context-related expertise contributes positively. Therefore, insights from these studies were each limited to a narrow span of a firm's strategy.

However, like firm strategies, board advice and counsel needs to be diverse and multilayered. It entails the evaluation of strategic plans and decisions, the analysis of drivers of firm value, and the discussion of different strategic options (Khanna et al., 2014; Zahra & Pearce, 1989). Jointly with the top management, directors reflect on new ideas and critique existing strategies to generate new and superior answers to present challenges (Daily & Dalton, 1992). To be effective, directors need to act as sound advisors for the many different and yet firm-specific problems a management team is facing. Moreover, directors need to be able to provide effective advice although they often lack superior knowledge about a certain aspect of a firm's business in several situations throughout their tenure.

Accordingly, the emphasis of board advice and counsel is less on developing alternative solutions based on superior knowledge but more on working with the firm's top management to reframe and enrich their problem solving. However, many prior studies implicitly assume that directors' advice-giving ability is grounded in declarative, content-based knowledge (e.g. knowledge about acquisitions or diversification) while overlooking the procedural and tacit aspects that strongly contribute to effective advice and counsel. As it is difficult to develop a theory on how different forms of directors' skills and knowledge impact a board's advisory function (Kor & Sundaramurthy, 2009; Tian et al., 2011) a comprehensive understanding of success factors of board advisory processes is still missing. With our investigation of director expertise which is more closely related to the advisory process, we partly close this gap.

Further, we provide a significant contribution to the sparse literature on board committees. Our study entails one of the very first tests of the effects of business related and strategy committees on firm performance. While most firms have implemented committees for audit, compensation, and nomination tasks, committees related to a firm's business activities are less frequent and rarely covered in empirical studies (Kaczmarek et al., 2012). We find that the presence of business committees positively affects firm performance. Based on our findings, we argue that boards which emphasize and improve their advice function with the formation of such committees will help to generate competitive advantages for the focal firm. The presence of business committees likely leads to a better structuring of the advisory process and helps to clarify responsibilities and coordination in the boardroom. It also makes it clearer to whom the CEO and other TMT members can refer to if they need advice on a business-related issue.

However, the non-significant effect of strategy committees warrants further explanation. Against our assumptions the formation of those committees seems to have no direct effect on firm performance. One likely reason could be that the tasks of strategy committees are defined too broadly. Discussions at those committees may not yield specific results but remain on the surface of strategic problems. In contrast, committees related to specific aspects of a firm's business are likely to produce more concrete results. Another reason could be that having a strategy committee signals a lack of strategic competence of the top management team because decisions regarding a firm's general strategy are one of their major responsibilities. Therefore, future research could more closely examine the role of strategy committees in connection with various firm and top management team characteristics.

Overall, our study highlights the relevance of board advice and counsel for the economic well-being of enterprises. Board involvement in strategic decision-making can be a crucial aspect of effective corporate governance. Directors who act as advisors help and encourage the TMT to improve continuously and to develop new strategies (McNulty & Pettigrew, 1999) and increase their influence on strategic processes and decisions (Dalton et al., 1998; Hillman & Dalziel, 2003). If boards are only concerned with monitoring and compliance-related issues, they may neglect the long-term perspective of a firm's strategy. For instance, there is often a discrepancy between shorter time horizons of CEOs and longer time horizons of board members. Some strategic decisions may exceed the retirement date of the current CEO and are, therefore, less likely to be addressed by him or her. Against the background of decreasing CEO tenures (Kaplan & Minton, 2012), boards must ensure that strategic planning aims at creating long-term firm value and is not affected by the shorter course of CEO tenures. Against this background, the clear separation of TMTs and corporate boards in strategic decision-making is increasingly tempered. For a greater part of their work, directors have become independent strategy advisors for the TMT of a firm. In the past, boards have occasionally been portrayed as rather passive "rubber stamps" of TMT proposals because of the high rates of uncritical approvals (McNulty & Pettigrew, 1999). More involvement in a firm's strategy and higher effectiveness of board advise-giving will help to overcome this view.

Despite our contributions to the literature, this study also holds some limitations that offer potential for future research. For instance, several other director characteristics might increase board effectiveness which we have not addressed. Although we controlled for the number of director ties, we do not take a director's social capital into account. However, prior research has revealed that a director's social connections outside and inside the firm can be important for effective board functioning (Hillman & Dalziel, 2003; Kor & Sundaramurthy, 2009). Moreover, other types of directors' human capital are likely to be valuable for advising a firm's top management. For instance, directors with specific knowledge, such as university professors or politicians, might provide valuable insights. Board heterogeneity and the interdependence of human and social capital have also been found to be important factors for the influence of boards on corporate strategies (Haynes & Hillman, 2010). Accordingly, future research should examine the best orchestration and balance of all these types of board capital.

In this study, we test direct effects of director expertise and board structures on firm performance. Our theoretical reasoning is to investigate factors which are relatively independent of specific problems or conditions. However, ample research shows that boundary conditions are important to understand board effects (Johnson et al., 2013). We want to note that we tested a set of boundary conditions of our results but found no relevant results. For instance, we examined whether the overall level of strategic change or the complexity of a firm's business affect the influence of advisory expertise, management expertise, or advisory-oriented board committees. Nevertheless, future research could further investigate how the board characteristics presented in this study interact with other firm and board-related characteristics.

We chose Tobin's Q as dependent variable because it ultimately captures effective advice and counsel. However, what could be of interest is a more proximate measure of advice and counsel excellence. For instance, questionnaires with CEOs and TMT members could provide meaningful insights into the perception of board advice at the top of the firm (Westphal, 1999). Similarly, future research needs to validate and eventually adapt theoretical models on board effectiveness on the basis of more process-oriented analysis. Although we do not observe board processes directly, we believe that the consideration of observable characteristics that can be assumed to capture the quality of board processes come as close as possible to a process-oriented view (Daily et al., 2003; Forbes & Milliken, 1999). Nevertheless, as with all studies using proxy variables to address unobservable constructs and relations, our insights into "real" processes in the boardroom are limited.

Lastly, we also assert that the traditional division of different board roles is far less clear than theory suggests. For instance, we show that board committees concerned with a firm's business have a positive and significant effect on Tobin's Q and argue that this is due to an improved and enhanced advisory process. However, it could also be the case that business-related committees help boards to evaluate strategic decisions of the TMT better, thus contributing to more effective monitoring. The ambivalence between monitoring and advice-giving provides an important avenue for future research. While there are attempts to integrate theoretical perspectives on different board roles (Hillman & Dalziel, 2003), overlaps and multiple dependencies between different board functions need to be examined in more detail to understand the drivers of board effectiveness.

Overall, the growing significance of boards as capable strategic advisors of a firm's management is mirrored in calls for research (McDonald et al., 2008; Pugliese et al., 2009) and concerns of practitioners (Bhagat et al., 2013; Nadler, 2004). However, this role has received only limited (empirical) attention so far. In light of increased volatility and complexity of international markets as well as recent financial and corporate crises, demands on corporate boards have heightened. Directors are expected to have a sound understanding of the strategic scope of a firm, to be actively engaged in challenging existing strategies, and to provide advice on future strategies. Our study of process-related director expertise and advisory-oriented board structures contributes to the knowledge on the prerequisites of effective board advice. We hope that our theoretical reasoning and empirical findings provide useful references for future research on the advice and counsel role of boards and its effects on firm performance and value creation.

3 Interpersonal Differences at the Top: The Case of CEO Non-duality and R&D Investment Strategy

3.1 Introduction

Governance research has largely neglected to examine the strategic role of the relationship between a firm's chief executive officer (CEO) and the chairman of the board (COB). Although the high relevance of this relation has been mentioned several times (Kakabadse, Kakabadse, & Knyght, 2010; Quigley & Hambrick, 2012; Roberts & Stiles, 1999). This is because in many countries, foremost the U.S., firms made use of the possibility to combine CEO and COB positions – the so-called CEO duality. Accordingly, research has focused on issues surrounding the question if CEO duality is beneficial for firms (Krause et al., 2014). However, research reviews conclude that there is no consistent positive effect of CEO duality (Dalton et al., 1998; Krause et al., 2014). Furthermore, CEO duality is no longer regarded to be a best practice for the leadership structure of firms (Lublin, 2012) and the percentage of firms that use CEO duality is constantly decreasing in many countries around the world[3]. Thus, the omission of research on the CEO-COB relation is surprising given the urgency for governance research to learn more about the case of CEO non-duality and the resulting relation of CEOs and COBs.

To address this gap in the literature, we develop a multi-theoretical framework to examine the effects of career and socio-personal differences between CEOs and COBs. To test our theoretical framework, we make use of a sample of the largest stock-listed firms in Germany where the local two-tier board system clearly separates management and supervisory functions. Firms within the German system are legally mandated to have a CEO as well as a separate COB. Thus, the empirical setting of Germany provides a unique opportunity to observe a complete sample of CEO-COB dyads which is unaffected by firm-level decisions either in favor or against CEO-duality.

---

3 In the U.S., for instance, the percentage of S&P 500 firms that separate the CEO and COB position raised from 20 percent in the early 90 s to almost 50 percent in 2015 (SpencerStuart, 2015).

Our theoretical framework adds a cognitive and social-psychological dimension to the CEO duality literature, which so far has largely relied on traditional theories of corporate governance, such as agency theory (Krause et al., 2014). In doing so, we follow and extend research that has examined the effects of personal differences between decision-makers at the top of the firm (Carpenter et al., 2004; Kor, 2006). This research has evolved around the assumption that different perspectives and heterogeneous backgrounds help teams to make better decisions and to be more innovative. Empirical results have confirmed this assumption with regard to more diverse TMTs (Bantel & Jackson, 1989; Hambrick, 2007; Naranjo-Gil, Hartmann, & Maas, 2008), heterogeneous director backgrounds (Haynes & Hillman, 2010), and the co-work of TMTs and corporate boards (Kor, 2006; Westphal, 1999). However, less is known about how characteristics of personal relations between TMT and board members affect a firm's strategic decisions (Boyd et al., 2011). Likewise, this research has often investigated the effects of many isolated characteristics but less so the effects of bundles of experiences and skills (Haynes & Hillman, 2010). Our theoretical framework addresses both research gaps. Moreover, many studies apply a static perspective on the relation of CEO and board member characteristics, ignoring that these relations evolve over time (Shen, 2003). We depart from this static view as we integrate a time dimension in our analysis of CEO-COB dyads and test how this time dimension moderates the effects of relational CEO-COB differences. To do so, we examine R&D investment strategies. R&D investments are on the one hand essential for a firm's overall competitiveness (Klingebiel & Rammer, 2014; Rumelt, Schendel, & Teece, 1994) and, on the other hand, in close proximity to the CEO-COB decision-making (Barker III & Mueller, 2002; Roberts & Stiles, 1999).

Overall, this study provides contributions for two avenues of research. First, we advance CEO duality research by putting light to the case of CEO non-duality and the largely neglected relationship between CEOs and COBs. Our theoretical framework helps to build knowledge about the dynamics of the CEO-COB relationship. Our research on relational effects of individual characteristics of CEOs and COBs addresses the "the issue with the greatest potential to generate insight, and yet with the least amount of research attention so far devoted to it" (Krause et al., 2014, p. 265) in research on CEO duality. We show that the relation of individual characteristics of CEOs and COBs has a substantial impact on a firm's R&D investment strategy. Further, by going beyond team-based measures and structural leadership characteristics, we follow calls for more fine-grained analyses in corporate governance research (Dalton & Dalton, 2010; Hambrick, Werder, & Zajac, 2008; Johnson et al., 2013). Second, our study addresses relevant gaps in the general research on differences at the top (Carpenter et al., 2004; Johnson et al., 2013) and contributes to a stream of literature that examines effects of top management and director characteristics on a firm's innovativeness (Alexiev, Jansen, Van den Bosch, & Volberda, 2010; Kor, 2006; Tuggle, Schnatterly, & Johnson, 2010; Zona, Zattoni, & Minichilli, 2013). We extend existing knowledge by showing that diverse and heterogeneous backgrounds not only are important for team decision-making but also for the relation between CEOs and COBs. Further, we provide new evidence on the differential effects of different types of experiences, demographic characteristics, and social backgrounds (Crossland, Zyung, Hiller, & Hambrick, 2014; Haynes & Hillman, 2010; Johnson et al., 2013) as well as on the role of contingency factors for strategic decision-making processes (Hambrick, Cho, & Ming-Jer, 1996; Zona et al., 2013).

3.2 Theory and Hypotheses

3.2.1 CEO-COB Relation and R&D Investment Strategy

In this paper, we are interested in the case of CEO non-duality and the effects of relational characteristics of CEO-COB dyads on a firm's R&D investment strategy. However, to understand the particular characteristics of the CEO-COB relation, it is important to consider that the majority of related research has focused on the issue of CEO duality. Relatively little research exist about the case of CEO non-duality and the resulting CEO-COB relation (Krause et al., 2014). For many years, research and practice favored CEO duality because of the potential positive effects on firm performance. However, in a meta-analysis, Dalton et al. (1998) were unable to find a direct link between CEO duality and firm performance and later research was likewise unable to find any consistent positive effect of CEO duality on a firm's economic well-being (Krause et al., 2014).

Our study departs from this research in two directions. First, we restrain from conducting another performance study but examine R&D investments as a more proximate outcome of CEO-COB decision-making. Second, we do not examine if CEO-COB separation itself is beneficial or not, but rather ask what characteristics in the CEO-COB relation are positive given that a separation of the CEO and COB position is in place. Thus, we provide a nuanced extension to the given CEO duality literature. Rather than asking whether separate CEO and COB positions are positive or negative, we examine what characteristics CEO-COB dyads must have to generate positive effects for a firm's orientation towards more innovativeness.

We examine R&D investments because R&D investment decisions are supposedly one of the most relevant decisions CEOs and COBs have to agree upon. For these highly relevant decisions, CEOs and COBs have to act as a team because the complexity and fast pace of issues to be solved exceed the problem-solving capacities of single individuals (Schweiger et al., 1989). R&D investments are the foundation of a firm's innovativeness and by that contribute essentially to a firm's market competitiveness (Barker III & Mueller, 2002). They are essential for the creation of new products and services (Brown & Eisenhardt, 1995; Klingebiel & Rammer, 2014), the development of absorptive capacity (Cohen & Levinthal, 1990), and other important prerequisites for sustained competitive advantage. On the other hand, underinvestment in R&D can severely harm a firm's capability to sustain in the market (Zona et al., 2013). Despite the importance of R&D investments for the long-term success, firms differ widely in their attention and dedication to R&D (Rumelt et al., 1994). Accordingly, understanding the antecedents of R&D investments is a fundamental question in strategic management.

In this context, the characteristics of top managers and board members as well as the configuration and quality of their interrelation have been shown to be important (Barker III & Mueller, 2002; Kor, 2006; Zona et al., 2013). However, despite the importance of R&D investments for a firm's long-term competitiveness, researcher note that managers often have a preference for restrained R&D strategies to reduce risks and to enhance short-term performance evaluations (Baysinger & Hoskisson, 1989; Baysinger, Kosnik, & Turk, 1991). Accordingly, the detection of top management and board related antecedents to more R&D investments is of high practical relevance. While strengthening corporate governance with the separation of the CEO-COB position itself has been shown to be a potential way to reduce the threat of underinvestment in R&D (Kor, 2006), we go one step further to examine how individual characteristics of CEOs and COBs interact in influencing a firm's R&D investment strategy.

3.2.2 Interpersonal Differences and Strategic Decision-making

Experiences and personal characteristics of a firm's top decision makers influence their way of thinking, their perceptions of the environment, and subsequently their decision-making (Carpenter et al., 2004; Cyert & March, 1963). Consequently, personal characteristics of a firm's top decision makers can have a relevant impact on the way organizations behave and perform (Finkelstein et al., 2009; Hambrick & Mason, 1984). Moreover, not only the personal characteristics of senior leaders can directly influence firm outcomes but also the relation of characteristics between team members and individuals in the upper ranks of the firm. To some degree, relational aspects are even more important as the direct impact of individuals (Hambrick, 2007). Looking at the relational side of personal characteristics and experiences of top executives and board members, an unresolved question is whether it is more beneficial if characteristics and experiences are relatively similar or relatively different.

On the one hand, a large body of literature on similarity in work relations suggests that similarity increases mutual liking and positive perceptions about others (Byrne, 1971; Singh & Ho, 2000), which, for instance, lead to higher chances of being promoted (Schaubroeck & Lam, 2002). However, studies also suggest that similarities in teams as well as in dyadic work relations, such as the CEO-COB relation, are positive for work outcomes. For instance, Westphal and Zajac (1995) show that when members of the board of directors are similar to a CEO, the board is more able to anticipate CEO decisions. In turn, alignment efforts are reduced. Besides the higher predictability of team member behavior, similarity also makes it easier to build trustful relations (Korsgaard, Schweiger, & Sapienza, 1995; Zhu & Westphal, 2014) and simplifies team interactions because shared experiences and similar patterns of thinking make it easier to understand each other (Michel & Hambrick, 1992; Ndofor, Sirmon, & He, 2015). Similarity also strengthens group commitment and cohesion (Harrison, Price, & Bell, 1998; Tsui, Egan, & O'Reilly III, 1992). Thus, there is some evidence that teams consisting of similar individuals could be more effective.

On the other hand, a large body of research suggests that differences in personal backgrounds within leadership teams bear several advantages. One of the most evident and well-documented outcomes of higher diversity in teams is the positive effect for creative tasks (Ancona & Caldwell, 1992). Functional dissimilar TMTs, for instance, increase a firm's innovativeness because of their broader perspectives, their higher ability to identify different solutions, and their increased communication (Bantel & Jackson, 1989). Likewise, heterogeneous boards are more flexible and have a higher inclination for strategic changes (Golden & Zajac, 2001). However, diverse backgrounds do not only influence the way strategic decisions are made but also the quality of decision-making in general. Educational heterogeneity, for instance, helps teams to transfer learning experiences to new and similar situations more successfully (Nadolska & Barkema, 2014). Governance research has commonly stressed the positive implications of complementary and collective leader characteristics for effective decision-making (Conger, Lawler III, & Finegold, 2001; Kor & Sundaramurthy, 2009).

Regarding the contradictory results of studies on similarity and differences, we first acknowledge that most likely both streams of literature are true with respect to their documented effects. However, in this paper, we argue that for the particular case of the dyadic CEO-COB relation and its impact on a firm's level of R&D investments, differences are more advantageous than high levels of similarity.

While some studies stressed the benefits of similarity between actors at the top, preferences for similar individuals are also often considered as a bias that harms effective decision-making (Tajfel & Turner, 2004; Zajac & Westphal, 1996). Overall, it could be argued that some of the above-mentioned benefits of more similarity, such as stronger commitment or a simplified communication, are even detrimental for more innovativeness. As creative and advanced problem-solving evolves through intense discussions and a reconciliation of different perspectives, simplified communication and strong commitment in homogenous teams could be disadvantages. Amason, Shrader, and Tompson (2006) point out that in close work relations with very frequent interactions, similarity between team members is helpful because it supports behavioral integration whereas loose work relations that imply gathering and integration of outside knowledge and information scanning benefit from heterogeneous backgrounds. As CEOs and COBs interact regularly but not very frequently and both roles involve providing broader perspectives that include scanning of a firm's environment (Parker, 1990), much speaks for the mentioned benefits of different backgrounds. Another example of the risks of high similarity comes from Allen (1977). In an early work on R&D innovations, he reports that engineers often restrain from seeking help and advice from other similar capable colleagues and partners because of their fear of skeptical reactions regarding their competencies. Thus, similarity can particularly inhibit R&D processes.

Furthermore, when COB and CEO positions are separated, the COB has a natural incentive to engage in a close relationship with the CEO to overcome potential information asymmetries. Thus, separation alone can trigger mutual exchange of information between a CEO and the board. This is assumed to increase board effectiveness for the benefit of the whole firm (Lorsch & MacIver, 1989). Researchers also argue that an active and vigilant board would prefer separate leadership positions to prevent CEO entrenchment (Finkelstein & D'aveni, 1994). When a COB and a CEO are very similar, it is easier for a CEO to align with the overseeing chairman, which, according to agency theorist assumptions, makes it easier for a CEO to minimize his or her risk exposure. However, as stated above, risk aversion is one of the dominant threats to innovations (Baysinger & Hoskisson, 1989; Baysinger et al., 1991). Thus, dissimilarity within a CEO-COB dyad could help to prevent CEOs from being too risk-averse.

To further develop our argumentation we follow calls for more theoretically derived measurements of individual characteristics in governance research (Johnson et al., 2013) and argue that the potential differences between a CEO and a COB can be best grouped into two categories – career differences and socio-personal differences. We will explore both categories in the following.

3.2.3 Career Differences

A common approach in research on director and executive characteristics is to group personal attributes into different categories. The use of aggregated measures that include multifaceted aspects of an underlying construct has been shown to be advantageous with regard to the study of differences and heterogeneity at the top of the firm (Haynes & Hillman, 2010). For instance, many studies refer to the categories of human and social capital (Kor & Sundaramurthy, 2009; Tian et al., 2011) or distinguish between experiences and demographics (Johnson et al., 2013). In the context of our study, we assume that the most useful categorization is into career-related experiences, which we will describe in the following, and socio-personal characteristics, which we address in the subsequent chapter.

The effect that different experiences of team members improve task performance seems to be very general (Littlepage et al., 1997). Thus, it will apply to a broad range of career-related experiences. Industry experience, for instance, is a critical resource for leadership teams (Kor & Misangyi, 2008). It has been observed that industry outsiders make mistakes in their strategic reactions to critical industry developments (Castanias & Helfat, 2001; Kor, 2003). Accordingly, the danger of wrong decisions or misinterpretations of industry trends is likely to be reduced when CEOs and COBs complement themselves in their industry knowledge. Especially with regard to R&D investment decisions, aspects such as scanning of the environment or knowledge and understanding of outside industry trends are important. Thus, different and complementing industry backgrounds likely provide benefits. It is also reported that dissimilar functional backgrounds can lead to higher team performance in innovative tasks. In a direct comparison, Bantel and Jackson (1989) found that banks with management teams that are dissimilar to each other with regard to their functional expertise were more innovative compared to those with more homogenous backgrounds. Hence, a COB with a different functional background could provide alternative perspectives to the CEO's decision-making and thus could broaden the scope for potential R&D investments.

A further aspect that is important to consider is that isolated types of career experiences can have ambiguous effects in the context of a firm's innovativeness. For instance, studies report that managers with a long firm tenure are valuable because of their insider and firm-specific knowledge, their familiarity with internal processes, and their rich networks within the firm (Harris & Helfat, 1997; Karaevli, 2007; Karaevli & Zajac, 2013). Accordingly, it is likely that high levels of insider knowledge support decision-making processes with regard to R&D investments. However, studies also report on the negative effects of a long tenure within a firm. Long-tenured insiders often rely on the status quo of the strategic orientation of a firm and pursue less strategic changes (Hambrick & Mason, 1984; Wiersema & Bantel, 1992). Moreover, insiders consider fewer alternatives and perspectives in their decision-making (Guthrie & Datta, 1997). Thus, long tenure could also inhibit the innovation process. This pattern of ambiguous effects of certain types of career experiences can also be applied to other experiences, such as the functional or industry background of an individual. These and other examples show that a combination of different levels of, for instance, insider and outsider knowledge or different functional backgrounds, could overall yield more positive effects compared to the presence of only homogenous backgrounds. Thus, dyads consisting of CEOs and COBs with divergent career backgrounds and therefore supplementing perspectives could overall increase a firm's innovativeness. Accordingly, we argue that:

Hypothesis 1:   *There is a positive relationship between the level of career differences between the CEO and the chairman of the board and R&D investments.*

3.2.4 Socio-personal Differences

We define socio-personal characteristics in distinction from career-related experiences described above as those characteristics of an individual that are not directly linked to his or her professional career track (Webber & Donahue, 2001). Decision-making researchers argue that the outcomes of group decision-making disputes depend on the type of group disagreements and discussions (Schweiger, Sandberg, & Ragan, 1986; Schweiger et al., 1989). Thus, we believe that it is necessary to distinguish between different sources of potentially opposing perspectives on problem-solving. Although one could assume that non-career related individual characteristics, such as demographics like age or gender, would have little influence on strategic decision-making (Naranjo-Gil et al., 2008), the opposite is true. Studies show that a broad range of different director and executive demographics directly influence firm outcomes (Finkelstein et al., 2009; Golden & Zajac, 2001; Johnson et al., 2013). The social and psychological characteristics of individuals are widely recognized as important factors of board and TMT decision-making (Cyert & March, 1963; Westphal & Fredrickson, 2001).

Differences in the demographic background and personal characteristics of decision-makers have shown, for instance, to lead to divergent preferences for related or unrelated diversification (Jensen & Zajac, 2004). Moreover, in their study of diversification strategies, Jensen and Zajac (2004) point out that these differential preferences are further moderated by structural components of leadership teams. Socio-psychological characteristics have also shown to influence the attention of decision-makers for certain issues (Tuggle et al., 2010). Thus, divergent socio-personal backgrounds might increase the potential range of issues that receive attention by a given CEO-COB dyad. Subsequently, options for R&D investments are likely increased as well. Social-psychological research also shows that people tend to believe more in their opinion to the extent that they have repeatedly expressed their position or have repeatedly been re-assured of it (Downing, Judd, & Brauer, 1992). When a CEO and COB are socio-personally similar, these kind of reassurances and repetitions of opinions are likely to be more frequent. However, it can be expected that, in turn, CEOs and COBs consider fewer alternatives and are subject to constrained perceptions about strategic choices. The opposite should apply for socio-personally different CEO-COB dyads.

Further, individuals with socially or personally diverse backgrounds can provide complementing perspectives to each other. In the board-TMT de-cision-making context, research shows that outsider perspectives increase advice and counsel interactions between top managers and board members (Carpenter & Westphal, 2001; Judge & Zeithaml, 1992). This leads to an increase in the number of available strategic options (Judge & Zeithaml, 1992) and broadens the accessible knowledge for strategic decisions (Johnson et al., 1996). Further, Schweiger et al. (1989) point out that deci-sion-making profit from integrating conflicts into the decision-making process. They particularly stress the benefits of processes such as dialectic inquiry and devil's advocacy, which we assume are more likely when the socio-personal backgrounds of CEOs and COBs are different. Therefore, we argue that:

Hypothesis 2:   *There is a positive relationship between the level of socio-personal differences between the CEO and the chairman of the board and R&D investments.*

3.2.5 Time Effects: The Role of Shared Tenure

In the context of CEO duality research, Boyd (1995) provided a seminal study that highlighted the role of contingency factors in the analysis of the effects of a certain leadership structure. He found that CEO duality only has a positive effect on firm performance when the environmental uncer-tainty for a given firm is high. Meanwhile, the contingency perspective is a central element to understand the effects of TMT or director characteris-tics on firm outcomes.

A highly important aspect of the relation between board members and a CEO is that relations are dynamic and change over time (Shen, 2003). Ac-cordingly, we assume that for our investigation of the effects of interper-sonal differences on R&D investment decisions, the shared tenure of a

CEO-COB dyad is an important factor. Shared experiences of working together are assumed to create a form of internal social capital that is possessed mutually by all members of a group (Adler & Kwon, 2002). Shared tenure likely enhances the knowledge about each other's expertise and deficits, of approaches to problem-solving, and other relevant aspects of the individual working style. Accordingly, researchers expect co-working experiences to be a strategic factor in team decision-making (Castanias & Helfat, 2001). Further, Kor (2003) and Kor and Sundaramurthy (2009) note that the combination of different types of experiences may diminish or amplify the unique effect of a particular experience. Therefore, we explore how the contingency of lower or higher shared tenure between a CEO and a COB might moderate the direct effects of career and socio-personal differences on R&D investments.

Shared tenure and career differences. The value of a certain knowledge or experience can diminish over time. This has already been shown, for instance, for the value of industry experience and expertise (Kor & Misangyi, 2008; Zald, 1969). Accordingly, we argue that the effect of career differences between a CEO and COB on a firm's R&D investments will be affected by the time a given CEO-COB dyad has been working together. As shared tenure increase, it is likely that common knowledge and the understanding of each other's expertise and cognitive perspectives also promote (Tian et al., 2011). This is valuable in the sense of the effectiveness of interactions and decision-making processes. However, the differences in expertise and cognitive perspectives and the associated discussions are exactly among those aspects which are expected to increase innovations (Bantel & Jackson, 1989; Kor, 2006). Thus, these effects are likely to be diminished when shared tenure increases.

Researchers also note that increased tenure comes at certain costs (Kor & Sundaramurthy, 2009). For instance, with higher tenure of directors, information exchange and communication is reduced, commitment to the status quo and avoidance of alternatives raises, and teams develop tendencies for groupthink (Boeker, 1997; Forbes & Milliken, 1999). Additionally, ongoing disagreements based on diverging professional perspectives can lead to fruitful discussion and improved decision-making but can also trigger destructive, relation-based conflicts (Jehn, 1997). Furthermore, actors often base their information exchange behavior on assumptions of reciprocity (Adler & Kwon, 2002), which means that they share knowledge and interact frequently when they assume that they can benefit from each other in the future. However, as shared tenure increase the benefits of sharing knowledge und seeking information are likely reduced because the incremental amount of new information the reciprocal partner can offer logically diminish over time. Accordingly, as the benefits of different career backgrounds diminish over time and meanwhile the risk of destructive conflicts increases, we argue that:

Hypothesis 3:   *The positive relationship between the level of career differences between the CEO and the chairman of the board and R&D investments becomes weaker as shared tenure increases.*

Shared tenure and socio-personal differences. As outlined above, we assume that socio-personal differences between a CEO and a COB lead to a higher orientation towards innovation and more R&D investments. However, if we add a time dimension based on the amount of shared tenure between a CEO and a COB, our assumptions are different for socio-personal differences compared to career-related differences. While we assume that the benefits of career differences diminish over time, we expect the opposite for the effects of socio-personal differences. That time can have differential effects for different types of diversity has already been proved, for instance, for the cohesion in work groups (Harrison et al., 1998).

In our case, we refer to the basic notice of psychological research that sociological and personality-based traits are among the most stable characteristics of individuals (Kassin, 2003). While the influence of past career experiences is maybe suppressed by more current conditions, socio-personal imprints more likely remain stable and present. Thus, we argue that the described moderating effect of shared tenure for career differences cannot be likewise applied to socio-personal differences.

Furthermore, based on socio-psychological research we assume another mechanism to be even more important in this context. Looking at the psychological side of the CEO-COB work relation, one has to consider that socio-personal differences can also diminish the quality of teamwork and decision-making because these differences can lead to conflicts and less efficient interactions (Amason, 1996; de Wit, Greer, & Jehn, 2012). Many studies that argue for the benefits of similarity directly or implicitly found their argumentation on the conflict potential of differences or the absence of conflicts based on high similarity (Byrne, 1971; Harrison et al., 1998; Ndofor et al., 2015). While we assume that the positive effects of different socio-personal perspectives outweigh potential disturbances based on conflicts, these effects are – nevertheless – likely to be present.

It is important to note that psychological theory suggests that the outcomes of conflicts in work settings depend on whether conflicts are constructive or destructive (Amason, 1996; Amason & Schweiger, 1997). Constructive conflicts emerge when individuals with different knowledge backgrounds and different cognitive perspectives work together on problems. These conflicts will encourage discussions, the challenging of existent beliefs and assumptions, and the consideration of new ideas. Prior research on constructive conflicts in top management and work teams show that it is beneficial for decision-making (Amason, 1996; Jehn, 1995) and that decisions profit from combining and exchanging different perspectives (Jehn & Mannix, 2001; Schweiger et al., 1989). In contrast, destructive conflicts are not task-related and based on non-rational arguments. Unlike constructive disputes, destructive conflicts are characterized by distrust, withhold of information, and reduced cooperation (Menon, Bharadwaj, & Howell, 1996). This leads to an inhibition of cognitive functioning and distracts individuals from their task-related problem-solving, leading to less and suboptimal decisions (Braiker & Kelley, 1979). If individuals perceive criticism and conflicts as based on personal rather than rational disagreement, conflicts become affective and destructive (Amason, 1996). Thus, dissimilarity in socio-personal characteristics will increase the likelihood of destructive conflicts and, in turn, likely reduces innovativeness (De Clercq, Thongpapanl, & Dimov, 2009). This is the more likely the case, the less familiar individuals are with each other (Fisher, 2012; Tsui & O'Reilly III, 1989).

However, if individuals share work experiences and engage in close interactions, precisely the problem of unfamiliarity is reduced (De Clercq et al., 2009). Accordingly, we assume that when shared tenure increases, destructive conflicts based on socio-personal differences are reduced. On the other hand, constructive conflicts based on those differences remain present because of the stability of socio-personal characteristics. Thus, in the case of a CEO and a COB with low levels of shared tenure and high levels of differences in their socio-personal background the likelihood of destructive conflicts should be high compared to the case when socio-personally different CEOs and COBs have high levels of shared work experience.

A further aspect is that strategic decisions often face time constraints and decision outcomes depend on the time it takes to come to a decision (Eisenhardt, 1989). As mentioned above, socio-personal differences can inhibit and slow down decision processes (Menon et al., 1996). However, as shared tenure increases, CEOs and COBs should become more effective in making timely decisions. Thus, delays or postponements of R&D decision should be less frequent, which in turn should increase the overall capacity for R&D investments. In sum, we assume that:

Hypothesis 4:   *The positive relationship between the level of socio-personal differences between the CEO and the chairman of the board and R&D investments becomes stronger as shared tenure increases.*

3.3 Methods

3.3.1 Sample and Data

In this study, we examine the influence of career and socio-personal differences between CEOs and COBs on R&D investments. The sample we use for this analysis covers dyads of CEOs and COBs from the largest stock-listed firms in Germany over a period of ten years from 2004 to 2013. To derive our sample, we use the HDAX index issued by the German stock exchange (Deutsche Börse AG) which consists of the 110 stock-listed firms with the highest market capitalization in Germany. As not all firms are consistently part of the HDAX over the whole period under study, we constrain our sample to include only firms that were part of the HDAX for at least three consecutive years.

Data in our study stem from two types of sources. Data on firm variables is largely obtained from the *Worldscope* database. For some firm variables, we complemented this data with information published directly by firms in their annual reports. For data on CEO and COB characteristics, we relied on carefully researched personal and career background information. To obtain as much information on CEOs and COBs as possible, we applied different search strategies. We integrated data on CEOs and COBs published by their firms, i.e. at corporate homepages or in annual reports, with data found on specialized websites, such as *Bloomberg executive profiles* or the *Munziger online archive,* and further sources, such as newspaper articles. In several cases, we also verified data by directly contacting firms.

For our analysis of the CEO and COB relation, the empirical context of Germany has some important characteristics that should be noted. The most important characteristic of the German context that supports our analysis of CEO-COB dyads is the fact that CEO duality is not allowed under the German Stock Corporation Law. The German two-tier board system separates the supervisory and the management function by not allowing executives of a firm to also serve on the respective supervisory board. Thus, COB and CEO positions are always held by different individuals and the only possibility for a CEO of a firm to become COB of the same firm is to resign as CEO. This clear separation creates a setting in which we can observe a two-person CEO-COB dyad for every firm in our sample[4].

Traditionally, the COB has a particularly strong position within German firms. Following the German Co-determination Law, half of all board members in large firms are employee representatives. Thus, in boards of large German firms, shareholder and employee representatives have in principle an equal voting power. However, within this system, the COB gets two votes if it comes to a situation of equality of votes. Thus, the COB can resolve critical voting situations based on his authority. Moreover, while the separation of the supervisory and the management function aims at setting a focus on strong monitoring, directors and top management team members in Germany also closely coordinate strategic decisions. The German Corporate Governance Code suggests that "The Management Board coordinates the enterprise's strategic approach with the Supervisory Board and discusses the current state of strategy implementation with the Supervisory Board at regular intervals" (Governance Commission, 2015, p. 4). Thus, COBs often closely monitor the decisions and behaviors of CEOs while at the same time are also engaged in providing advice and counsel. Typically, the intensity of interactions between COBs and CEOs is high. Therefore, the characteristics and the quality of the CEO-COB relationship should be of high relevance for a firm's strategic decision, such as the level of R&D investments.

3.3.2 Variables

Dependent variable. We measure a firm's level of innovativeness with R&D investments. While many studies on innovation rely on some type of intensity measure and assess a firm's innovativeness as R&D investments

---

4 We excluded the very few cases where a firm had two CEOs at the same time.

divided by total sales, total assets, or number of employees (Chen, 2014), authors note that each of these standardizations hold problems concerning potential distortions of the true innovative power of a company. For instance, Hitt, Hoskisson, and Kim (1997) note that R&D measures based on standardization on, for instance, firm sales can produce problems due to a non-natural relation of such measures to firm size. Therefore, we follow studies that use the mere level of R&D investments as an undistorted measure of a firm's innovativeness (Balkin, Markman, & Gomez-Mejia, 2000; Graves & Langowitz, 1993). We control for the potential effect that larger firms have higher levels of R&D investments by including firm size as a control variable in our regression models.

Independent variables. The independent variables career differences and socio-personal differences are both composite measures consisting of a number of indicators that assess distinct differences between CEOs and COBs. The composite measure *career differences* is based on four indicators. We assess whether CEOs and COBs are different with respect to the field of their education, their dominant industry background, their dominant functional background, or their level of firm outsiderness. These characteristics are typical indicators of executives' or directors' career-related experiences (Crossland et al., 2014; Johnson et al., 2013) and provide a comprehensive coverage of the career path of a CEO or a COB.

Following Wiersema and Bantel (1992), we measure whether CEOs and COBs received their *education* in either business/economics, engineering, sciences, law, or liberal arts. Differences in the educational background imply different perspectives and skill-sets (Nadolska & Barkema, 2014). The field of a person's higher education can influence many later career decisions. Education also affects the way investment decisions are evaluated (Hambrick et al., 1996; Wiersema & Bantel, 1992). Thus, differences in the educational background between CEOs and COBs could directly impact how R&D investment decisions are made.

To assess a CEOs or COBs *dominant industry background,* we examined all firms and respective industries a CEO or COB has worked in during his or her career. We then identified the industry in which a CEO or COB has spent the largest amount of years. This industry was then considered the dominant industry background of a CEO or COB. We measure the industry background of a CEO or COB based on the Global Industry Classification Standard retrieved from Worldscope, which categorizes firms into ten different industry sectors (Crossland et al., 2014). As industries vary in their characteristics, they provide highly divergent career and work settings. Accordingly, industry knowledge is crucial because it enables decision-makers to anticipate new developments in technology, the competitive landscape, customer or supplier behavior, and other important and path-dependent industry-specific characteristics (Boeker, 1997; Castanias & Helfat, 2001; Kor & Misangyi, 2008). It has further been shown that differential and thus complementing industry backgrounds can be a critical factor in strategic decision-making (Kor & Misangyi, 2008).

Our measure of the *dominant functional background* is based on eight different categories (Cannella, Park, & Lee, 2008) which are management/administration, production/operations, engineering/R&D, accounting/finance, personnel/labor relations, marketing/sales, law, and others. Similar to the industry background variable, we assess in which of these eight different functions a CEO or COB has spent most of his or her career. Many studies assume that the functional background of a director or an executive is one of the most formative influences for decision-making (Cannella et al., 2008; Carpenter et al., 2004; Forbes & Milliken, 1999). Moreover, research also shows that functional dissimilarity in teams can be linked to increased innovativeness (Bantel & Jackson, 1989).

We also assess whether CEOs and COBs are more outsiders or insiders with respect to the firm they are currently heading. The number of years a manager or director has worked within a firm is a well-known antecedent for many strategic decisions (Finkelstein et al., 2009). Long-tenured managers are, for instance, assumed to be more risk-averse when it comes to decisions regarding corporate change or R&D investments (Kor, 2006). A further common finding is that firms with outsider CEOs pursue more strategic change compared to firms with insider CEOs (Boeker, 1997; Shen & Cannella, 2002). Therefore, we created the dummy variable *firm outsiderness* that is 1 if a CEO/COB has a high level of firm outsiderness and 0 if a CEO/COB has a low level of firm outsiderness. To do so, we defined a CEO/COB to have a high level of firm outsiderness (a low level of insider knowledge) if he or she has spent fewer years within the current firm as the average CEO/COB in our sample. Correspondingly, we defined a CEO/COB to have a low level of firm outsiderness (a high level of insider knowledge) if he or she has spent more years within the current firm as the average CEO/COB in our sample. This approach has been applied in similar studies on TMT members' level of experience within a firm (Wiersema & Bantel, 1992). It is also in line with more recent studies that highlight the importance to apply more refined measures of outsiderness (Karaevli, 2007; Karaevli & Zajac, 2013) to capture the true and relative level of familiarity with a firm compared to often arbitrarily defined cut-offs in years.

For all these four career background characteristics our assessment of a difference between a CEO and a COB is straightforward. CEOs and COBs are different in the respective characteristic if they do not share the same type of background. For instance, a CEO and a COB have a similar dominant functional background if they both worked for the largest part of their career in a marketing or sales function but are different if they have dominantly worked in different functions. They are different in their education if they have received their education in different fields. They are different regarding their dominant industry background if they have spent the largest part of their careers in different industries. Further, they are different in their level of outsiderness, if one has a high level of outsiderness (compared to the sample average) and the other has a low level of outsiderness (compared to the sample average).

Similarly to the composite measure of career differences, we also assess the socio-personal background of CEOs and COBs. The composite measure *socio-personal differences* is also based on four distinct differences. We measure whether CEOs and COBs are different with respect to their highest level of education, their national origin, their age, and their foreign experiences. We are aware that beyond these four, there are further potential indicators for the socio-personal background of an individual. However, information on other as the named characteristics is often difficult to obtain. For instance, we tried to assess the socio-economic background of CEOs and COBs. However, information on the socio-economic background is often unavailable or unreliable. Accordingly, this and several other potential indicators of the socio-personal background of CEOs and COBs could not be incorporated due to data unavailability. Furthermore, some characteristics, such as gender or ethnic minority status, were not considered because of the very low frequency of occurrence in our sample of German firms. Nevertheless, it can be considered that the four examined characteristics provide an adequate and valid assessment of the level of socio-personal differences between a CEO and a COB. All these four indicators have been shown to influence the cognitions and behaviors of individuals and represent some of the most commonly used variables in studies on executive and board member backgrounds (Carpenter et al., 2004; Johnson et al., 2013).

For our first indicator of socio-personal differences, the *level of education*, we assess whether CEOs or COBs have a secondary educational degree (such as a master or diploma title) or not. As most executives and directors have some secondary educational degree, having no secondary educational degree is a relevant and apparent differentiation and thus a strong indicator of a socio-personal difference between a CEO and a COB. CEOs and COBs are different in their level of education if one has a secondary educational degree while the other has not. The level of education has already been used in other studies on director and executive characteristics as an indicator of differences between individuals at the top (Finkelstein et al., 2009; Zhu & Westphal, 2014). It is assumed to be one of the most salient indicators of status which affects group interactions and individual perceptions (Westphal & Bednar, 2005).

The variable *national origin* is based on the nationality of a CEO or COB as indicated in theirCV. Thus, a difference in this indicator means that a CEO and a COB are of different nationalities. If we were unable to find precise information on a CEOs or COBs nationality, we looked at the country of a CEO's or COB's place of birth instead. Nationality or place of birth are closely linked to the ethnic background of individuals. Both, nationality and the ethnic background have been shown to influence board and TMT processes and to influence firm outcomes directly (van Veen & Elbertsen, 2008; Westphal & Milton, 2000). Our third indicator, *foreign experience*, addresses a similar background characteristics. It measures if CEOs or COBs have spent significant amounts of time (at least two years) during their adult life in a country different from the country they have spent their childhood. Thus, a CEO and COB are different with respect to their foreign experience if one has experienced to live in a foreign country while the other hasn't.

Our fourth indicator of socio-personal differences, *age*, is measured as the number of years since birth. While slight differences in age are unlikely to have a relevant effect on the co-work of CEOs and COBs, larger differences in age highly shape an individual's social background and are therefore a relevant source of differences. If individuals belong to different age cohorts, they have experienced different political and social environments during their life and have experienced different phases of economic development (Bantel & Jackson, 1989). Furthermore, Westphal and Zajac (1995, p. 64) note that "differences in age can create the perception of dissimilarity, independent of underlying attitudinal or behavioral differences." However, to define a certain amount of years to be a relevant age difference is difficult. Thus, we only rated CEOs and COBs to be different in their age if the age difference between them is larger than one standard deviation from the mean age difference between CEOs and COBs in our sample. Thus, we use the sample as a reference and rate relevant deviations from the sample as a relevant age difference.

Beyond the direct effects of career and socio-personal differences on a firm's level of R&D investments, we argue that the interaction of career and socio-personal differences with the shared tenure of a CEO and a COB also affect a firm's level of innovativeness. The variable *shared tenure* is measured as the number of years a given CEO-COB dyad has worked together in the constellation as CEO and COB of the respective firm. We do not count the overall number of years two individuals have worked together within the same firm because spending years in the same firm does not imply the kind of close work relation that is typical for the CEO-COB relationship.

Control variables. We control for several variables at the industry, firm, and individual level that might influence a firm's level of R&D investments. At the firm level, we control for *firm size* (number of employees) because larger firms usually have more scope to facilitate innovations (Damanpour, 2010). We control for *firm age* (years since foundation) because younger, more entrepreneurial firms could, for instance, have a stronger inclination for R&D investments compared to more mature corporations. We also control for *board size* (number of directors) as well as for *prior firm performance*. Prior firm performance is calculated as the average return on assets (ROA) of the three previous years. If data were unavailable for all three previous years, we used time frames of two or one years instead. Further, we control for the *leverage* of a firm, measured as the ratio of total debts to total assets, because firms with a higher leverage could have more discretion to exhibit higher R&D investments. The level of R&D investments, which we use as a measure of a firm's level of innovativeness, might vary with respect to different industries. Typically, firms in some industries have higher levels of R&D investments, e.g. pharmaceutical firms, while others have lower levels of R&D investments, e.g. financial service firms. Thus, to control for industry effects, industry dummies were included in all regression models. Additionally, we control for the *industry adjusted performance* of a firm in the current year calculated as the deviation of the ROA of the respective firm from the industry mean. We also control for *industry growth* measured as the three years growth rate in sales for the respective industry. At the individual level, the variable *chairman CEO experience* assesses whether COBs were CEOs at any time during their career. Recent research shows that whether COBs are former CEOs or not influence subsequent strategic decisions and firm out-comes (Quigley & Hambrick, 2012). In our case, this could affect our as-sumptions on the impact of career differences because COBs which have experienced the role of a CEO within their career will have a much closer understanding of the perspectives of CEOs and, thus, potential differences in the career background could be less influential. We also control for po-tential effects of the number of years a CEO-COB dyad is present in our sample. Thus, we count the *frequency of dyads*. Lastly, year dummies were included in all regression models. Year and industry dummies are not displayed in the regression table.

3.3.3 Data Analysis

In this study, we test if career or social-personal differences between CEOs and COBs influence a firm's level of innovativeness and if shared tenure moderates these effects. To test our assumptions on the effects of career and socio-personal differences between CEOs and COBs, we apply a random effects model with maximum likelihood estimation. A Haus-man-test (Hausman, 1978; Wooldridge, 2009) confirmed that, given our data, a random effects model is a valid and appropriate choice compared to a fixed effects model. The maximum likelihood estimation requires more restrictive assumptions, for instance, regarding the distribution of variables and is more efficient compared to a least squares estimation if the underlying data is unbalanced (Crossland & Hambrick, 2007). In our case, the dataset is unbalanced because it contains firm observations with varying numbers of year observations. Moreover, for large samples, the it-erative approach of the maximum likelihood estimator leads to more effi-ciency compared to non-iterative single step estimates because it accounts for the relative magnitude of the variance components (Roquebert, Phillips, & Westfall, 1996).

A common problem in multiple regression analysis is multicollinearity. To test whether our models are affected by multicollinearity, we calculated variance inflation factors (VIFs) for all variables in our models. The aver-age VIF for all variables is 2.31 and the highest VIF for a single variable is 7.46. Thus, all VIFs are below the value of 10, which is assumed as a critical cut-off for potential problems of multicollinearity (Kutner et al., 2004). Using data from the defined panel of HDAX firms, we hierarchi-cally test our hypotheses. Results of these tests are described in the following section. Interaction effects are tested, visualized, and interpreted with standard procedures suggested in the context of multiple regression analysis in management research (Aiken & West, 1991; Dawson, 2014).

3.4 Results

Descriptive statistics and correlations for all variables are displayed in Table 3. Overall, correlations between variables are low to moderate, except for the correlation between board and firm size and shared tenure and frequency of dyads which both are higher than 0.6. The high correlation between board and firm size is explained by the fact that the size of German boards is by law bounded to the size of the firm. The high correlation between shared tenure and frequency of dyads is logical because every year a dyad is present in our sample increases the shared tenure between the respective CEO and COB.

Table 4 presents the results of the analysis of career and socio-personal differences between CEOs and COBs and R&D investments. In Table 4, Model 1 reports only control variables, whereas Models 2 to 5 present a hierarchical test of our hypothesized effects. Precisely, Model 2 shows the results for the hypothesized direct effects of career and socio-personal differences on R&D investments. In Model 3 and 4 the hypothesized interactions with shared tenure are added and Model 5 presents the results of a full analysis of direct and interaction effects.

Our first hypothesis predicted that a high level of differences in the career background between CEOs and COBs lead to more R&D investments. Likewise, with hypothesis 2, we predicted that high levels of differences in the socio-personal background of CEOs and COBs positively impact R&D investments. Model 2 in Table 4 shows that these two hypotheses are supported by our data. The effect of career differences as well as the effect of socio-personal differences are positive and significant (*career differences* $\beta = 0.037$, $p < .10$; *socio-personal differences* $\beta = 0.060$, $p < .01$). In Model 3, we added the interaction effect of career differences and shared tenure. Results show that the interaction is negative and significant ($\beta = -0.034$, $p < .05$). In contrast to the negative interaction of career differences and shared tenure, we predicted that the interaction of socio-personal differences and shared tenure is positive. Results in Model 4 show that our prediction is strongly supported. The interaction effect of socio-personal differences and shared tenure is positive and significant ($\beta =$

0.060, $p < .001$). Model 5 shows results for the full model including direct and interaction effects. In the full model, both, direct effects (*career differences* $\beta = 0.042$, $p < .05$; *socio-personal differences* $\beta = 0.081$, $p < .001$) and interaction effects (*career differences*shared tenure* $\beta = -0.034$, $p < .05$; *socio-personal differences*shared tenure* $\beta = 0.060$, $p < .001$) are significant. Figures 1 and 2 show interaction graphs for the two interaction effects of career differences and socio-personal differences with shared tenure.

Table 3: Descriptive Statistics and Correlations (Study 2)

Variable	Mean	SD	1	2	3	4	5	6	7	8	9	10	11	12
1 R&D investments	0.08	1.10												
2 Firm size[a]	9.52	1.81	0.55											
3 Firm age[a]	3.96	1.02	0.07	0.40										
4 Prior firm performance	6.12	7.78	-0.07	-0.07	0.14									
5 Leverage	2.65	1.33	0.16	0.33	0.06	-0.12								
6 Industry growth	10.00	17.51	-0.01	-0.13	-0.11	0.02	-0.04							
7 Industry adjusted performance	1.09	8.66	-0.04	-0.05	0.14	0.51	-0.24	0.07						
8 Board size	12.52	5.34	0.43	0.76	0.37	-0.18	0.24	-0.14	-0.14					
9 Frequency of dyads	5.17	2.67	-0.03	-0.04	0.01	0.06	0.04	-0.02	0.16	-0.12				
10 Shared tenure (st)	3.21	3.07	-0.08	-0.18	-0.12	0.14	-0.10	0.06	0.16	-0.25	0.61			
11 Chairman CEO experience	0.63	0.48	0.14	0.24	0.12	0.07	-0.08	-0.08	0.08	0.22	0.07	0.02		
12 Career differences	2.52	0.92	-0.09	0.02	-0.01	0.00	0.08	0.01	-0.00	-0.11	-0.05	-0.04	-0.17	
13 Socio-personal differences	1.56	0.96	0.23	0.13	-0.15	-0.10	0.09	-0.06	-0.02	0.11	0.03	0.03	0.19	0.01

$N = 580$; all correlations greater than $|0.08|$ are significant at $p < 0.05$. [a] Variables are log-transformed.

Table 4: Effects of Career and Socio-personal Differences on R&D Investments

Variable	Model 1	Model 2	Model 3	Model 4	Model 5
Firm size	0.701***	0.689***	0.698***	0.690***	0.699***
	(0.090)	(0.090)	(0.089)	(0.089)	(0.089)
Firm age	-0.317***	-0.308***	-0.312***	-0.301***	-0.305***
	(0.083)	(0.083)	(0.082)	(0.082)	(0.082)
Prior firm performance	0.019	0.013	0.011	0.002	0.000
	(0.026)	(0.025)	(0.025)	(0.025)	(0.025)
Leverage	0.015	0.006	0.004	-0.000	-0.002
	(0.027)	(0.027)	(0.027)	(0.027)	(0.027)
Industry growth	0.044	0.041	0.041	0.039	0.039
	(0.031)	(0.030)	(0.030)	(0.030)	(0.030)
Industry adjusted performance	0.003	0.001	-0.001	-0.002	-0.004
	(0.019)	(0.019)	(0.019)	(0.019)	(0.019)
Board size	-0.001	0.021	0.023	0.021	0.023
	(0.060)	(0.060)	(0.060)	(0.060)	(0.059)
Frequency of dyads	-0.009	-0.011	-0.007	-0.011	-0.007
	(0.026)	(0.025)	(0.025)	(0.025)	(0.025)
Shared tenure (st)	0.026	0.028	0.028	0.029+	0.029+
	(0.018)	(0.018)	(0.018)	(0.018)	(0.018)
Chairman CEO experience	0.046	0.056	0.052	0.066	0.061
	(0.043)	(0.044)	(0.044)	(0.043)	(0.043)
Years	Y	Y	Y	Y	Y
Industry	Y	Y	Y	Y	Y
Career differences		0.037+	0.038*	0.042*	0.042*
		(0.019)	(0.019)	(0.019)	(0.019)
Socio-personal differences		0.060**	0.061**	0.080***	0.081***
		(0.021)	(0.021)	(0.022)	(0.022)
Career differences X st			-0.034*		-0.034*
			(0.016)		(0.016)
Socio-personal differences X st				0.060***	0.060***
				(0.018)	(0.018)
Constant	0.659	0.597	0.614	0.535	0.553
	(0.453)	(0.450)	(0.448)	(0.447)	(0.445)
Observations	580	580	580	580	580
Number of firms	79	79	79	79	79
chi2	106.09***	117.92***	122.33***	129.35***	133.80***

*** $p<0.001$, ** $p<0.01$, * $p<0.05$, + $p<0.1$. Two-tailed hypotheses tests. Coefficients for year and industry dummy variables are not reported.

Figure 1: Interaction Effect of Career Differences and Shared Tenure on R&D Investments

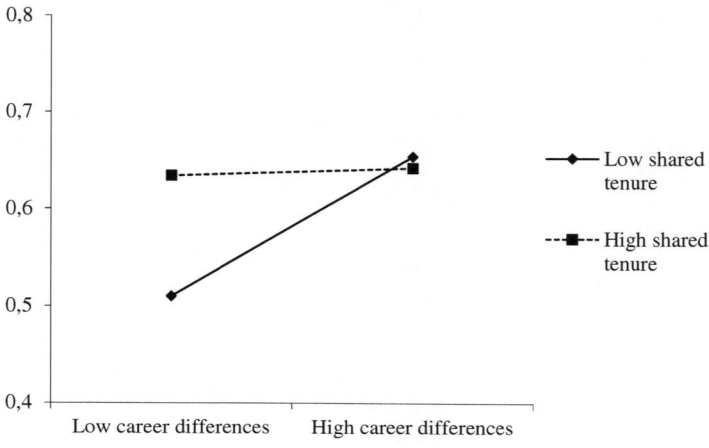

Figure 2: Interaction Effect of Socio-personal Differences and Shared Tenure on R&D Investments

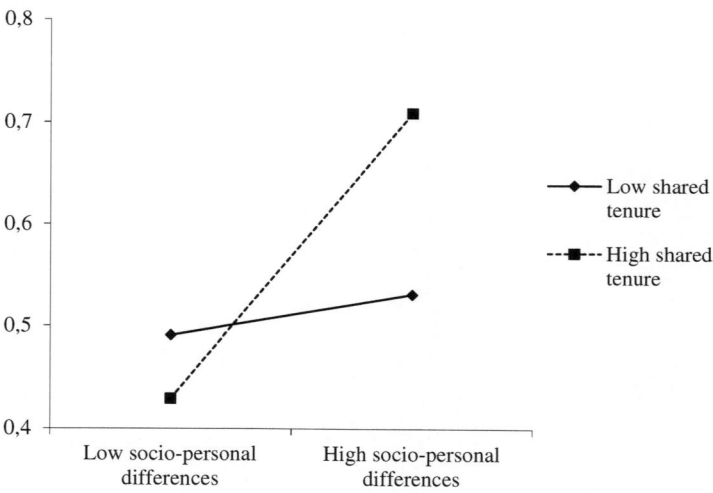

3.5 Discussion

If CEO and COB positions are separated, personal characteristics of the individuals holding these positions can vary. However, prior research has largely focused on the potential benefits of CEO duality and has almost ignored the case of CEO non-duality and the relational effects of individual characteristics of CEOs and COBs (Krause et al., 2014). This led us to the question how far interpersonal differences between a CEO and a COB might influence important firm decisions. We analyze interpersonal differences in the context of R&D investments as an essential resource allocation decision CEOs and COBs have to agree upon. We follow a rich stream of research that stipulates that for firms to foster innovations different and complementary perspectives of decision makers are superior compared to homogenous backgrounds (Ancona & Caldwell, 1992; Bantel & Jackson, 1989; Kor, 2006; Zona et al., 2013). Using a sample of the largest stock-listed firms in Germany, where CEO duality is prohibited, we can observe a full sample of CEO-COB dyads. Specifically, we investigate the relationship between CEOs and COBs concerning their career and socio-personal differences. Our results reveal that differences between CEOs and COBs in their background characteristics whether they are socio-personal or career-related generally foster R&D investments. With our data at hand, we can conclude that for the case of CEO non-duality, interpersonal differences between CEOs and COBs seem to be a fruitful ground for a higher level of innovativeness.

However, we also find that shared tenure is a significant moderator of these effects. Familiarity and shared experiences as important factors in team and dyadic decision-making (Huckman, Staats, & Upton, 2009; Tuggle et al., 2010) seem to influence the direct effects of CEO-COB differences. Our results show that the benefits of career differences not only diminish when shared tenure increases but turn around to become negative. Our interpretation of this effect is as follows. At the beginning of a CEO-COB relation, different career perspectives foster constructive discussions and thus lead to a higher orientation towards R&D investments. However, as shared tenure increases, perspectives of CEOs and COBs likely become more assimilated as they are increasingly shaped by similar experiences in the current setting of the firm. We believe that although their perspectives become more similar, CEOs and COBs might still find that they have very different and yet open-minded and constructive views on a firm's R&D strategy. Accordingly, they might underestimate their constrained views of the business environment and become highly prone to stick to the status quo – a common effect of a long tenure (Wiersema & Bantel, 1992; Wu, Levitas, & Priem, 2005). In turn, this might reduce their efforts towards innovations and could explain the negative interaction effect we observed.

As the composition and structure of top leadership positions have received high attention in research as well as in practice (Finkelstein et al., 2009; Krause et al., 2014), our results provide important implications for future research, public debates, and practical leadership decisions in firms. According to our results, COBs should be selected upon their individual qualifications and personal background characteristics. Thereby, firms should take into consideration how the qualifications and individual characteristics of a COB can complement the perspectives of a CEO to foster the quality of strategic decisions. This is also relevant for the case of CEO selection. In selecting CEOs, boards often tend to have a bias towards candidates that are similar to themselves both regarding career backgrounds as well as in their personal background (Westphal & Zajac, 1995; Zhu & Westphal, 2014). According to our results, this bias can be a threat for the innovativeness of firms. Boards and COBs should be aware of the potential bias to prefer similar candidates and should look for candidates that might challenge their assumptions and perspectives. Our results also provide implications for research on the practice of relay-succession (Brickley, Coles, & Jarrell, 1997; Shen & Cannella, 2003). If firms reward successful CEOs by appointing them as chairman after their active service as CEO, firms could indirectly create a threat to their innovativeness. In the case of a relay succession, the likelihoods for having a CEO-COB dyad with similar experiences can be assumed to be significantly higher compared to a non-relay succession.

Our results also have implications for other related research on director and TMT characteristics. For instance, some researchers also define shared tenure as a type of social capital (Tian et al., 2011). Thus, one could argue that a higher mutual social capital (through increased shared tenure) of CEOs and COBs further increases the positive effects social diversity but diminishes the effects of career related differences as part of the human capital of CEOs and COBs. These effects would be thus an interesting avenue for future research on interactions of social and human capital (Haynes & Hillman, 2010) and distinctions between external and internal social capital (Tian et al., 2011).

The study also provides implications for research on board monitoring. An additional explanation of the positive effect of differences between

CEOs and COBs on R&D spending could be that COBs who are different from a CEO are more motivated to engage in active monitoring and thus help to prevent risk-aversion strategies that diminish R&D investments. Agency theory suggests that the more independent a board member is, the higher his or her motivation to monitor (Fama & Jensen, 1983). Being different could be a factor that increases the perceived independence and, in turn, lead to an increase in motivation to monitor. We also want to stress that the relation of a CEO and a COB is not only in itself important for the R&D decision-making process but has implications for the whole group of top managers and directors at a firm. Research on decision-making in small groups contends that dyadic relations can have effects on larger groups via processes of social conformity and behavior imitation (Hackman, 1992). These effects are supposedly especially strong for the CEO-COB dyad. Further, future research could extend our findings by examining in more detail the complementary perspectives of CEOs and COBs. In our study, we relied on composite measures of the overall differences in career and socio-personal characteristics. Therefore, a logic refinement of our results would be to examine how certain single attributes influence the decision-making process of CEOs and COBs. For instance, a functional background in R&D could have a distinct effect.

A potential limitation of our study is the generalizability of our results to corporate governance settings in which CEO duality is allowed. In one-tier corporate governance systems, such as the U.S., CEO and chairman positions can be obtained by the same person. However, our results are still of great importance for these governance systems. Several studies address the potential benefits and downsides of CEO duality (Dalton et al., 1998). Our results show that having a COB and a CEO with different career or socio-personal backgrounds can be beneficial for a firm's innovativeness. Therefore, firms in one-tier governance settings might want to divide COB and CEO positions to benefit from the advantages revealed in our study. The reduced number of firms in the U.S. that establish CEO duality (SpencerStuart, 2015) points to a trend that firms start to recognize the distinct benefits of CEO non-duality.

Our study is also subject to a common problem in research on the effects of executive or director characteristics on firm outcomes which is that firm outcomes are usually influenced by a set of many different factors. This makes it difficult to establish rigorous theoretical explanations in how far certain characteristics influence a particular outcome. However, for some firm outcomes, such as firm performance, the link to executive or director characteristics is likely more indirect as for others. R&D investment decisions presumably fall into the second category. Nevertheless, a limitation of our study is that we were not able to directly observe or review the actual process of R&D investment decisions. Future research could, therefore, refine our findings by analyzing in more detail the exact processes by which differences between CEOs and COBs influence strategic decisions.

4 Corporate Governance between Shareholder Value and Stakeholder Orientation: Lessons from Germany

4.1 Introduction

Over the last decades, the optimal governance of corporations and the inherent benefits and downsides of different corporate governance systems around the world have received substantial attention (Aguilera & Jackson, 2010; Cappelli, Singh, Singh, & Useem, 2010; Khanna, Kogan, & Palepu, 2006). One of the most recurring elements of interest is whether governance systems converge to a shareholder value model and if shareholder value models are superior over other, more stakeholder-oriented conceptions of corporate governance (Allen et al., 2015; Shleifer & Vishny, 1997). However, while empirical evidence and well-developed theoretical models for both, shareholder- and stakeholder-oriented views exist (Donaldson & Preston, 1995; Jensen, 2002; Laplume, Sonpar, & Litz, 2008), the debate about the superiority of either model is ongoing. Conclusive answers in terms of comparative effectiveness and efficiency as well as the influence either model has on firm outcomes such as performance is therefore still lacking.

In practice, shareholder models have dominated for many years as a point of reference for adapting governance systems geared towards higher competitiveness. This consensus on a shareholder-oriented model is not only widespread in the Anglo-Saxon countries, where it originated, but has also gained growing worldwide influence due to the success of contemporary firms operating under this system. Furthermore, the global spread of the academic disciplines of economics and finance as well as the diffusion of share ownership in many developed countries have contributed to the dominance of this model (Hansmann & Kraakman, 2000). However, a number of recent corporate scandals in the U.S., the collapse of Lehman Brothers, and the following financial crisis have raised doubts about the superiority of the Anglo-Saxon shareholder-centered model of corporate governance. These events revealed inherent vulnerabilities of a strictly shareholder-oriented governance conceptualization and have renewed interest in alternative models.

Attention to this debate is further enhanced by constitutive differences in the dominating theoretical models underlying both paradigms. Shareholder value conceptions, which proclaim profit maximization for shareholders as the only objective of firms (Jensen, 2002), draw mainly on agency theory (Jensen & Meckling, 1976), assuming that corporate constituencies seek to maximize their respective value at the expense of others if effective control mechanisms do not prevent self-interested behavior. In contrast, stakeholder approaches rely more on ethical views and resource-based approaches (Freeman, 1984; Freeman, Wicks, & Parmar, 2004). Especially instrumental stakeholder theory (Donaldson & Preston, 1995; Jones, 1995) and a body of related empirical work (e.g. Kacperczyk, 2009; Ogden & Watson, 1999) have established an alternative theoretical framework to analyze stakeholder relations. Focusing on the positive impacts of stakeholder management on organizational outcomes such as innovations or financial performance (Harrison & Wicks, 2013; Hillman & Keim, 2001; Verbeke & Tung, 2013), this stream of research has revealed new insights on the benefits of stakeholder orientation. Constructive stakeholder relations are perceived as valuable because they provide access to or represent important resources (Harrison et al., 2010). Thus, in light of a global convergence towards the Anglo-American model of shareholder orientation (Yoshikawa & Rasheed, 2009), the question arises, if and via what mechanisms the cooperative approach to stakeholder relations and subsequent stakeholder management in stakeholder-oriented corporate governance systems also hold advantages for firms.

We seek to address this research gap with a closer look at Germany's corporate governance. Our aim is to show that in its current mixture of incorporated shareholder value practices and an institutionalized stakeholder-oriented rationale, Germany's corporate governance can be considered as a form of advanced and modern stakeholder value approach. We believe Germany to be a particularly interesting setting to examine questions concerning the effects of stakeholder orientation and management for several reasons. First, Germany has often been criticized for its stakeholder-centered conception of corporate governance. Portrayed as the sick man of the euro, the German model was predicted to fail (Economist, 1999). Due to criticism raised on the traditional stakeholder model, several shareholder-oriented practices were introduced during the 1990 s – sometimes against initial resistance of different institutional forces (Sanders & Tuschke, 2007). Nowadays, (shareholder) value-oriented performance measures are routinely used in German firms. However, they are rather seen as instruments of corporate planning and managerial accounting than as the sole purpose or number one goal of the firm. While German firms have introduced shareholder-oriented practices (Fiss & Zajac, 2004; Tuschke & Sanders, 2003), they are still embedded in an institutional setting characterized by strong stakeholder rights, cooperation between corporate constituencies, and a coordinated market economy (Capron & Guillén, 2009; Hall & Soskice, 2001). In contrast to companies from shareholder-oriented governance systems, German firms tend to manage the interests of their key stakeholders more actively, in particular those of large owners and employees. The resulting stakeholder management is highly institutionalized and anchored in laws, social rules, and norms. Thus, German firms usually exhibit a very active stakeholder management (Jürgens et al., 2000). While the German economy has regained its economic strength, critics remain and point to the need to understand the relative utility of different elements of Germany's corporate governance and its implications for other governance systems. Due to these reasons, our study fills a research gap of prior studies which have analyzed the advantages of stakeholder-oriented governance systems only with regard to firm outcomes rather than analyzing in detail the mechanisms associated with specific designs of stakeholder orientation (Harrison & Wicks, 2013; Hillman & Keim, 2001; Verbeke & Tung, 2013).

Beyond the specifics of Germany, we suggest that research on the instrumental value of stakeholder orientation at the level of national corporate governance is very timely. Considering that the degree of stakeholder orientation is one of the most prominent differences between national corporate governance systems (Aguilera & Jackson, 2003), a better understanding of the role of more or less stakeholder orientation of corporate governance systems is essential. It serves the growing interest in stakeholder value models as an alternative to purely shareholder-oriented governance (Aguilera et al., 2008). In this respect, a more fine-grained knowledge of the pros and cons of different corporate governance conceptualizations and a broader understanding of valuable resources for firms that operate in networks of stakeholder and shareholders relations seem beneficial. Against this background, we discuss positive outcomes but also challenges of the stakeholder value orientation of German firms. We try to show that Germany is evolving towards a modern stakeholder value approach that aims at answering the needs of global capital markets and at decreasing problems associated with traditional stakeholder approaches, like power imbalance or a lack of transparency.

Our analysis of Germany's current corporate governance contributes to different streams of literature. First, we add to research on the variety of different corporate governance systems (Aguilera & Jackson, 2010) and their effects on firm behavior and firm outcomes (Chang, Oh, Park, & Jang, 2015; Griffiths & Zammuto, 2005). We also contribute to the literature on pros and cons of stakeholder management in general (Harrison et al., 2010; Verbeke & Tung, 2013). By doing so, we also answer calls for a reorientation within stakeholder theory to examine the impacts of stakeholder management on broader concepts of firm performance (Laplume et al., 2008) and continue the theoretical debate about shareholder and stakeholder value (Freeman, Harrison, Wicks, Parmar, & De Colle, 2010; Hillman & Keim, 2001). Lastly, we continue a smaller stream of literature on the specifics of Germany's corporate governance and the surrounding debates (e.g. Fauver & Fuerst, 2006; Fiss & Zajac, 2004; Sanders & Tuschke, 2007) by covering the latest status of Germany's corporate governance and its position within the large framework of different corporate governance systems around the globe.

4.2 International Corporate Governance and the Shareholder vs. Stakeholder Debate

Interest in the effects of national corporate governance settings on the competitiveness of firms is not limited to Germany. With the global expansion of financial and product markets and an increased exposure of domestic firms to international competition, a growing concern about the role of country-level institutions for industry or firm-level competitiveness has generally emerged in most countries across the world as they look to each other for potential advantages and disadvantages of national corporate governance systems (Aguilera et al., 2008; Christmann, Day, & Yip, 2000). Accordingly, scholars in this line of research call for a more in-depth view that advances the understanding of processes and conditions by which national institutions impact firm-level outcomes (Aguilera & Jackson, 2010; van Essen, van Oosterhout, & Heugens, 2013).

A starting point for this research is to understand in what ways national corporate governance systems vary and how a particular corporate governance system, like Germany, can be classified along different dimensions. While many such classification schemes exist, research on corporate governance has largely relied on those that classify the governance systems of developed market economies. Analyses focus on Anglo-Saxon countries, Europe, or Japan (Kaplan, 1997; Surroca & Tribó, 2008) and examine characteristics such as the board system, the relevance of capital markets, or the ownership structures of firms (Shleifer & Vishny, 1997). For example, Weimer and Pape (1999, p. 154) provide an extensive taxonomy of national systems of corporate governance by differentiating between Anglo-Saxon, Germanic, Latin, and Japan as country classes of corporate governance systems.

Beyond classifications based on individual characteristics, the most commonly used approach in management literature is to categorize countries as shareholder- or stakeholder-oriented. This classification approach is holistic and therefore in some ways more useful than others because the relative orientation towards shareholder versus stakeholder interest groups influences nearly all aspects of corporate governance. While this classification is used to simplify the comparison of different systems, it is worth to note that there is potential variation of firm behavior within national corporate governance systems. Several firms in shareholder-oriented countries, like the U.S., explicitly follow a stakeholder-oriented approach in contrast to the prevailing shareholder value model. Likewise, firms in stakeholder-oriented countries can also pursue a strong shareholder-oriented management approach.

Despite the existing variation of firm behavior within countries, national corporate governance systems differ in the way they regulate rights, obligations, and relations of different actors with a stake in the firm based on historical developments (Aguilera & Jackson, 2003; O'Sullivan, 2000). These differences empower or constrain the influence stakeholders can impose over decision-making and resource allocation within a firm and highly predispose the degree and modality of interaction between them (Aguilera & Jackson, 2003). Such differences are often rooted in formal laws and conventions as well as in informal norms and values and thus represent institutional settings which are relatively persistent (Capron & Guillén, 2009).

Shareholder-oriented countries are characterized by a strong protection of shareholder rights, which particularly cover those holding only minority shares. Shareholder power is strengthened by active markets for corporate control, a dependence of firms on financing through capital markets, and clear transparency regulations (Hall & Soskice, 2001; La Porta, Lopez-de-Silanes, & Shleifer, 1999). In those countries, other stakeholders of the firm often have fewer claims when it comes to control over decisions and assets. For instance, the influence of employees is often relatively weak due to highly flexible labor markets (van Essen et al., 2013). Prime examples of shareholder-oriented systems are the United States and other Anglo-Saxon countries. On the contrary, in stakeholder-oriented governance systems, rights of different stakeholder groups are more equally distributed. With legal regulations or social conventions to integrate different stakeholders into firm governance and decision-making, Germany and other stakeholder-oriented countries such as Japan are often mentioned as alternative models to the Anglo-American conception (Jackson, 2001; Kaplan, 1997).

The categorization into shareholder- or stakeholder-oriented governance is accompanied by two partly opposing paradigms which influence and shape corporate governance systems around the world. Tracing back to early disputes about the purpose of privately held corporations and the conflicts arising from separation of ownership and control (Berle & Means, 1932), the shareholder value maximization paradigm proclaims that the most efficient way for managers to create value is to focus primarily on the interests of shareholders (Fama & Jensen, 1983; Jensen & Meckling, 1976). These claims were debated in research as well as practice very early on. For instance, in 1919, auto magnate Henry Ford lost a famous lawsuit in which he tried to defend his approach to withhold dividends for the benefit of stakeholders other than his shareholders in line with his view that business should also serve society (Lee, 2008). Just years later, in the 1930 s, Berle's famous claim for shareholder orientation was criticized by his colleague Merrick Dodd who suggested that business and corporate managers have responsibility for society beyond the interest of owners and therefore should engage in social responsibility (Dodd, 1932).

Nevertheless, shareholder value models dominated the public discussion at least in Anglo-Saxon countries. Potential solutions to align the interests of managers and shareholders, for example by the introduction of stock-option pay, were at the center of corporate governance debates throughout the second half of the 20th century (Jensen & Murphy, 1990; Shleifer & Vishny, 1997). Based on the general assumption that firms should pursue profit maximization as their "single-valued objective" (Jensen, 2002, p. 237), advocates of the shareholder perspective see stakeholder obligations as detrimental to firm success. In this view, managerial attention to stakeholders and stakeholder influence on firm strategy leads to inefficient resource allocations, impaired decision-making, and reduced accountability of managers (Aguilera & Jackson, 2010; Jensen & Meckling, 1976). Engaging for instance in corporate social responsibility activities was assumed to be a symptom of an agency conflict because managers would use such activities to strengthen their positions at the expense of shareholders (Friedman, 1970). Managers who try to concentrate on multiple interest groups at the same time are expected to end up in unresolvable conflicts, leading them to make flawed decisions, which finally result in diminished value creation for all stakeholders (Jensen, 2002). Accordingly, the stakeholder orientation of German firms could reduce their competitiveness relative to firms from shareholder-oriented governance settings, which are free to concentrate their efforts on shareholder interests (Williamson, 1985). Moreover, in shareholder models, rights and interests of non-shareholding stakeholders are assumed to be completely covered by existing contracts with the firm (Fama & Jensen, 1983; Jensen & Meckling, 1976). Thus, firm management should exhibit only limited motivation to devote additional attention to their needs. If this applies, a tradition of devoting much attention to stakeholders – as it is the case in Germany and other stakeholder-oriented countries – should be an excessive burden and would not provide any additional value for firms.

On the other hand, the stakeholder paradigm disagrees with several assumptions made in shareholder value models. It suggests that balancing the interest of different stakeholders, including non-shareholders, is superior with regard to overall value creation (Donaldson & Preston, 1995; Freeman, 1984; Freeman et al., 2010). Rather than focusing on a single objective, firms should acknowledge that "each group of stakeholders merits consideration for its own sake and not merely because of its ability to further the interests of some other group, such as the shareowners" (Donaldson & Preston, 1995, p. 67). Placing the interest of one group (i.e., shareholders) above all others is assumed to take place at the expense of those who receive less attention (Donaldson & Preston, 1995). It is further argued that through balancing interests and pursuing multiple objectives, firms are better able to increase value, which in the end sustains overall welfare for all constituencies of the firm (Freeman et al., 2004; Jones, 1995). Stakeholder orientation is said to be associated with reduced costs in the long-run, due to a reduced need for control – e.g., through less information asymmetries – and more efficient transactions (Freeman, 1984). Most importantly, attention to stakeholders is expected to secure access to valuable resources beyond what is offered on the basis of contracts (Barney & Hansen, 1994; Harrison et al., 2010; Hillman & Keim, 2001).

In contrast to shareholder models, it is also argued that attention to stakeholders not generally hamper the interest of shareholders. Non-normative stakeholder models such as the instrumental stakeholder theory already take shareholder interests into account, as part of a wider stakeholder perspective (Freeman et al., 2004; Jones, 1995). Consequently, the underlying assumption of many business studies – i.e., that the interests of shareholders and (other) stakeholders are generally in conflict – can be challenged. Moreover, the instrumental view deems the interests of stakeholders (including shareholders) as largely overlapping because each stakeholder group is to a greater or lesser extent dependent on all other stakeholders (Harrison & Wicks, 2013). Seeing corporate governance through this lens, firms in stakeholder-oriented governance settings might not suffer from their stakeholder orientation, as traditional agency- or shareholder-oriented models would assume, but instead ameliorate their competitiveness through constructive stakeholder relations.

Before we proceed with the analysis of Germany's stakeholder-oriented corporate governance system, we want to emphasize that not all existing stakeholder relations are explicitly addressed. Although early stakeholder theorists labeled stakeholders as any "group or individual who can affect or is affected by the achievement of the organization's objectives" (Freeman, 1984, p. 46), most current studies embrace a more nuanced definition of stakeholders depending on the given problem or context at hand (Capron & Guillén, 2009; Harrison et al., 2010; Hillman & Keim, 2001; Walsh, 2005). Likewise, we focus on stakeholders at the firm-level that can exert significant influence over asset control, decision-making, and resource allocation (Aguilera & Jackson, 2003). Other stakeholder groups such as customers or the society at large are only indirectly addressed.

4.3 Corporate Governance in Germany

Stakeholder orientation in Germany has a long history. After the end of the Second World War, the rebuilt state authorities of Western Germany installed a model of a social market economy which combined elements of free market economies with strong social welfare systems and high coordination of market actors (van Hook, 2004). Subsequently, the power of central stakeholder groups, in particular those of employees, was strengthened in two phases (Fohlin, 2005). In 1951 the government introduced the Cooperative Management Law (Montan-Mitbestimmungsgesetz) which set the ground for the cooperative approach to shareholder and employee rights in the governance of stock-listed firms. Later, in the 1970 s, the Co-determination Law (Mitbestimmungsgesetz) further solidified the role of employee representatives.

After the fall of the Iron Curtain in 1990 and the reunification of Germany, German firms tried to introduce a more shareholder-oriented management style in reaction to pressures from the internationalization of capital and product markets (Tuschke & Sanders, 2003). Influenced by the Anglo-American model of shareholder value, the introduction of stock-based compensation of executives, transparent accounting standards, and a general shift towards more market-based control systems aimed at increasing competitiveness in global markets (Fiss & Zajac, 2004; Sanders & Tuschke, 2007). During this time, some researchers expected a convergence towards the Anglo-American governance model of shareholder orientation (Yoshikawa & Rasheed, 2009). However, the introduction of shareholder-oriented practices often violated the dominant institutional logic in Germany (Sanders & Tuschke, 2007). Although German firms were increasingly embedded in institutional contexts outside of Germany and therefore amenable to market-oriented changes, the society at large, as well as legislative forces, were more reluctant. Many suspected the introduction of shareholder-oriented practices to go at the expense of other stakeholder groups and therefore acted to preserve the traditional norms and values of an egalitarian governance model. Thus, the central characteristics of the traditional stakeholder model, such as co-determination regulations, have endured all transformations (Tuschke & Luber, 2012).

Figure 3: Legislative Adjustments to Germany's Corporate Governance between 1950 and 2015

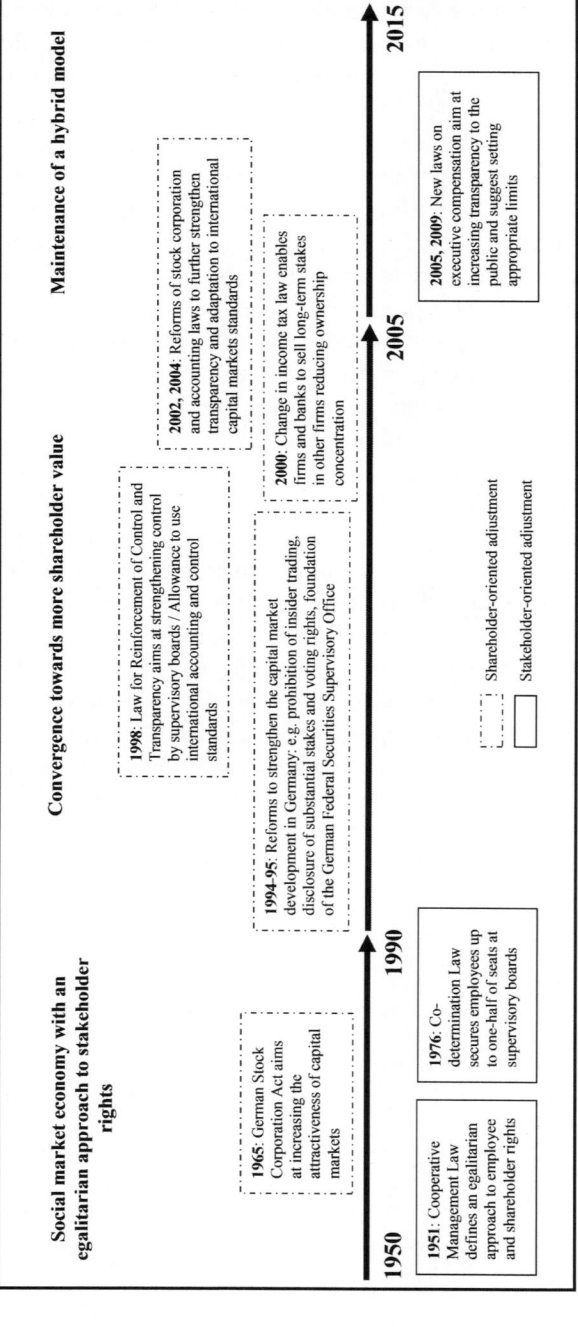

One of the persisting traditional characteristics of Germany's corporate governance is the separation of the supervisory and management functions through a two-tier board structure. It consists of a management board – akin to the top management team in U.S. firms – and a supervisory board that can be compared to outside directors in the U.S. (Fiss & Zajac, 2004). The management board defines and implements strategies, leads firm operations, and reports to the supervisory board. The German supervisory board is responsible for monitoring long-term strategy and executive performance, appointing and dismissing the CEO, and setting compensation for top management team members. Unlike in the Anglo-American governance system, members of the management board are not allowed to serve on the supervisory board. With its clear distinction between decision-making and decision control, the two-tier system provides German supervisory boards with a stronger monitoring focus than their Anglo-American counterparts. Thus, stronger board monitoring serves as a balance for weaker control from capital markets.

Another distinct feature of Germany's corporate governance is that the supervisory board is subject to employee co-determination. Up to one-half of the seats on the supervisory board of listed firms are legally reserved for employee and union representatives. Consequently, employees have a say in monitoring and advising relevant strategic and governance decisions made at the top of the firm. That is further strengthened by the general presence of highly organized works councils in nearly all larger firms (Mueller, 2012). Potential conflicts arising from the strong representation of employees at supervisory boards are partly reduced by a legal mandate for the chairman of the board to mediate conflicting interests between employee and shareholder representatives (Interessenausgleich). In a similar vein, the strong monitoring focus of German boards is attenuated by the living practice of close relations, intense communication, and consensus seeking between the chairman, other members of the board, and the top management team (Aguilera & Jackson, 2003).

Germany's corporate governance is also characterized by its relatively concentrated ownership structure, compared to countries with highly developed capital markets, like the U.S. (Thomsen, Pedersen, & Kvist, 2006). Groups of strategically oriented blockholders such as banks, family owners, or other corporations enforce strong influence over many firms in Germany (Tuschke & Luber, 2012). These blockholders tend to show greater commitment to a particular firm than other shareholders. For instance, banks frequently show greater involvement in a firm's strategic decision-making than other financial investors because they are interested in stable and long-term relationships with a firm to keep a vital creditor relationship alive (Jackson & Moerke, 2005). Thus, they display an overlap of interests as both shareholders and business partners of a firm. Especially the role of banks as investors has been a dominant characteristic of Germany's corporate governance while it is also visible in other stakeholder-oriented countries, such as Japan (Jackson, 2001). Although state ownership is no longer widespread in German firms, there are some notable exceptions such as Volkswagen, which is governed through an unusual hybrid of family control, government ownership, and labor influence. Here, the German state of Lower Saxony holds 20 percent of voting shares. Another prominent example is Deutsche Telekom, which was formerly 100 percent state-owned and where the German Federal Government still holds 14.3 percent of shares.

Family ownership, which is frequent even within the largest German firms and very common among small and medium-sized firms (Andres, 2008), shows similar patterns. As family firms are often managed by founders or their relatives, a concurrence of management and ownership is typical (Fama & Jensen, 1983; Hutchinson, 1995). Here, interests of family owners go beyond short-term profits to include a more sustainable perspective on firm control, development, and survival (James, 1999). Family firms are also characterized by close relationships with stakeholders and strong embeddedness in networks of local communities (Gomez-Mejia, Cruz, Berrone, & De Castro, 2011). Thus, as large owners in German firms are often involved in a firm's strategic planning and decision-making, they tend to emphasize long-term interests. In return, firms have to recognize the particularly strong influence of large owners and possibly take their interests into account. That can create two-way interest relations resulting in cooperative approaches in which blockholders as important stakeholders of the firm receive additional attention in return for their engagement.

Overlapping interests also used to be a characteristic of the dense network of relations between German firms referred to as "Germany Inc.". German firms were highly related through multiple cross-holdings (La Porta et al., 1999; Windolf & Beyer, 1996). Over the last years, however, these dense relations have increasingly dissolved (Heinze, 2004). Similarly, executives of larger German firms tended to serve on supervisory boards of other firms and German directors regularly held seats on the boards of several firms. That created strong social relations between firms through multiple board interlocks. The slowly resolving but still existing network of overlapping relations is said to be associated with a long-term alignment of strategic goals, higher levels of cooperation, and protection against external interventions such as hostile takeovers (Tuschke & Luber, 2012; Windolf & Beyer, 1996). However, in line with findings from previous research that board interlocks lead to the establishment of a cohesive "corporate elite" accountable only to themselves (Useem, 1984), German corporate governance legislation has aimed to reduce the amount of interlocks. For example, by limiting the number of boards an individual director is allowed to serve on.

A further typical element of the German economy which is associated with Germany's stakeholder orientation is the strong presence of small and medium-sized enterprises (SMEs). A significant portion of these firms are controlled by a majority of members of the same family or a small group of families, thus showing a close link to the characteristics of family firms. Although a strong sector of SMEs is not directly related to the German governance model, its existence has wider implications for the general role of different stakeholders in Germany. Similar to family firms, SMEs are traditionally highly rooted in stakeholder relations and exhibit quite strong commitment to various stakeholders (Berghoff, 2006).

The typical elements of Germany's corporate governance, a two-tier board system, employee co-determination, concentrated ownership with a large proportion of blockholders, dense networks of business and social relations between firms, the common presence of family ownership, and a strong sector of SMEs and industrial firms demonstrate that stakeholder orientation and stakeholder management are deeply anchored in Germany's economy. Accordingly, stakeholder orientation in Germany can be considered to be highly institutionalized. As firms are not only constricted by the legislative framework but also by the structure and characteristics of the institutional environment, corporate governance regulations as well as common practices and traditions directly shape firm-level decisions (Aguilera & Jackson, 2003; Dacin, Goodstein, & Scott, 2002). According to institutional theory, institutionalized activities are rooted in values and habits, corporate culture, shared beliefs or social rules and represent socially accepted conditions, which are relatively resistant to change and tend to persist even if rewards or advantages of their existence diminish (Dacin et al., 2002; Oliver, 1992). Thus, irrespective of shareholder-oriented changes in corporate governance regulations, German firms pursue an active management of influential stakeholder groups, including awareness and monitoring of stakeholder interests in strategic planning to anticipate effects on firm strategies.

As mentioned in the beginning, shareholder value models would assume that boundedness of German firms to stakeholders should weaken their competitiveness compared to firms from countries with more shareholder-friendly governance systems. However, insights from the instrumental stakeholder view and literature on the value of stakeholder management as a source of competitive advantage challenge such models of the firm (Harrison et al., 2010). Although stakeholder orientation might not be a source of competitive advantage per se, it could be argued that firms in such settings can create competitive advantage through active management of stakeholder relations. This might occur parallel to typical conflicts that arise from strong stakeholder orientation.

4.4 Stakeholder Orientation as a Source of Competitive Advantage?

Stakeholder theory has early on stressed potential advantages for firms that follow a stakeholder-oriented management approach (Freeman, 1984). Meanwhile, a growing number of empirical studies support the basic notion that firms whose managers take a stakeholder-oriented approach can outperform those who do not (e.g. Berman, Wicks, Kotha, & Jones, 1999; Hillman & Keim, 2001; Kacperczyk, 2009). In one of the first studies, Ogden and Watson (1999) found that, although more stakeholder orientation is costly for firms, it can lead to an increase in shareholder value. Likewise, Berrone, Surroca, and Tribó (2007) explain how stronger inclinations of firms to act ethically in stakeholder relations increases stakeholder satisfaction which subsequently leads to better firm performance. Later studies advanced the understanding of the positive relation between stakeholder management and firm performance by showing, for instance, that stakeholder orientation can be beneficial because managers – against the assumptions of the shareholder value perspective - engage in more long-term and value-oriented strategies when pressures of capital markets are reduced (Kacperczyk, 2009). Other scholars have pointed out that stakeholder management not only increases goodwill of stakeholders but also leads to the reduction of risk-associated costs (Godfrey, 2005). Additionally, a large body of studies on the effects of corporate social responsibility has found that even those activities that benefit stakeholder groups which are not directly involved with a firm, such as social communities, can lead to positive firm outcomes (Aguinis & Glavas, 2012; Margolis & Walsh, 2003).

Based on this broad empirical basis, the evolving instrumental stream within stakeholder theory has gained considerable momentum. It builds on the assumption that "firms that contract (through their managers) with their stakeholders on the basis of mutual trust and cooperation will have a competitive advantage over firms that do not" (Jones, 1995, p. 422). Thus, rather than solely focusing on ethical issues often stressed in normative stakeholder theories, the instrumental view concentrates on achievements relevant for performance. It tries to resolve the usual tension between ethical viewpoints and needs for performance optimization.

Scholars using the instrumental perspective dig into processes by which different stakeholders provide or represent important resources for the firm. Many studies in this field base their theoretical models on the assumptions of the resource-based view of the firm (Barney, 1991; Barney & Clark, 2007). It argues that differences in the competitive advantage of firms in the same industry or product market can be traced back to differences in the access, configuration, and combination of resources (Black & Boal, 1994). Thereby, advantages that are socially complex, have a high path dependency, and are ambiguous in their causality are considered to be more sustainable because they are hard to imitate by competitors (Barney & Clark, 2007). As discussed before, stakeholder orientation in Germany is highly rooted in social rules and norms. It can be considered to be a historically grown, socially embedded, and for outsiders often vague construct. Thus, German stakeholder orientation could fulfill several important prerequisites of a sustainable competitive advantage. Moreover, structurally complex, intangible resources like legitimacy, knowledge creation, or trust that contribute to a competitive advantage because they are hard to imitate are particularly influenced by positive stakeholder relations (Barney & Hansen, 1994; Dyer & Hatch, 2006; Hillman & Keim, 2001).

However, against the background of the resource-based view, positive-sum relationships to employees, owners, and other stakeholders only contribute to a firm's competitive advantage in so far as they are superior to those created by other firms. Stronger orientation towards stakeholders will not automatically lead to improved firm outcomes. On the contrary, strong stakeholder groups that are not managed adequately can even diminish firm performance because those stakeholders can detract created values (Coff, 1999). Actors in business relations are only cooperative to the degree they perceive a relationship to be fair in the way inputs and out-

comes are distributed (Adams, 1965; Hosmer & Kiewitz, 2005). Stakeholder relations are sensitive not only to the final distribution of value but
to the process by which the distribution is negotiated and decided
(Phillips, Freeman, & Wicks, 2003). Overall, it can be argued that "a
consistent stakeholder management strategy is likely to be more competitive than a strategy that 'picks and chooses' the stakeholders it wants to
treat well." (Harrison et al., 2010, p. 67). Thus, the success of stakeholder
management depends greatly on the quality of existing relations. Firms
that are able to create stakeholder management strategies that secure adequate information sharing, perceived fairness and respect in interactions
as well as relative parity in value distribution are likely to profit more
from stakeholder relations than competitors who are less able to do so
(Harrison et al., 2010).

4.5 Benefits of Stakeholder Orientation in Germany

The tradition of stakeholder orientation in Germany provides a positive
ground for fair relations. A crucial aspect is worker co-determination. Although worker co-determination is sometimes associated with reduced decision-making quality (Gorton & Schmid, 2004), others point out that
there is no one-way relationship between co-determination and the quality
and effectiveness of strategic decisions (Fauver & Fuerst, 2006). The value of worker co-determination may depend – even more than other stakeholder relations – on the quality of the relation itself. Co-determination
might only be beneficial in a setting where it can contribute to an increase
in trust, commitment, and motivation.

In market- and shareholder-oriented governance settings, employees are
among those stakeholder groups with the lowest influence on strategic decisions and therefore often have to take the greatest cutbacks within
change processes (Griffiths & Zammuto, 2005). This makes positive reactions and respective contributions of employees to change processes less
likely. In contrast, the German corporate governance setting highly pro-
tects workers' rights and provides an institutionalized frame for engaging
them in firm decision-making. This can make a major difference when it
comes to strategic adaptations that occur at the expense of employees. Extant research shows that the success of change initiatives greatly depends
on attitudes and reactions of employees (Kotter & Cohen, 2002). For instance, the participation of employees in strategic change initiatives is said

to reduce resistance and to increase commitment (Lines, 2004). Participation may also foster the willingness to accept temporary personal losses to help a firm to survive.

This kind of positive outcomes of co-determination in reaction to organizational crises and intensive strategic change can be regularly observed in Germany. For instance, the German car manufacturer Opel was about to go bankrupt in 2008 (Handelsblatt, 2008). In the face of bankruptcy, union and employee representatives, the top management of Opel as well as the local state government negotiated an egalitarian solution. Bankruptcy could finally be avoided because employees accepted substantial wage reductions and payment in shares in exchange for job security (Der Spiegel, 2009). This solution would hardly have been achieved without the strong voice and position of employee representatives and the willingness to co-operate even in light of a severe crisis. While in the aftermath of the 2008 financial crisis car producers around the world filed for bankruptcy or had to merge with competitors to survive, the German automotive industry – although currently suffering from spill-over effects of the Volkswagen scandal – endured this phase with the help of various stakeholder groups (Tagesschau, 2011). This shows that co-determination and the general way of stakeholder management in German firms increase trustful relations between owners, managers, and employees and therefore can add to the stability and long-term competitiveness of German firms. Moreover, it reveals the benefits of a broader social legitimacy of stakeholder-oriented management whose positive effects also have been confirmed by empirical studies (Heugens, van den Bosch, & van Riel, 2002). They are also visible in other stakeholder-oriented governance systems, such as Japan, where the close networks between firms and different stakeholders groups show similar patterns of high embeddedness (Jackson & Moerke, 2005).

The active management of employee relations can also be an important channel of improved learning and innovation outcomes for firms. To stay innovative, firms must constantly seek to increase their ability to integrate, recombine, or detect valuable knowledge from inside as well as outside the organization (Lewin, Massini, & Carine, 2011). However, learning and innovation processes are often characterized by bounded rationality and limited perceptions about the best way of adapting the firm to changes in the business environment (Greve, 2003). These challenges can be mitigated by accessing nuanced information from stakeholders. Co-determination through board seats or works councils, for instance, is associated with reduced information asymmetries and more information exchange between firm management and employees (Fauver & Fuerst, 2006). This can lead to an improved use of existing internal knowledge as well as an enhancement of learning opportunities because employees often have closer access to and a better understanding of the firm's products and customer needs.

Another aspect in this context is the ability of firms to learn constantly over time. Due to a more egalitarian approach in many German firms, employees stay with one firm for a longer period. Moreover, as shown by Turban and Greening (1997), paying attention to stakeholder interests makes firms more attractive to highly skilled employees, which are considered to be an important aspect of sustainable competitive advantage (Colbert, 2004). Indeed, German firms build their competitiveness often on a highly experienced workforce (Culpepper, 1999). Consequently, based on trustful and stable relations, employees are more willing to increase their firm-specific skills and knowledge and are thus better able to contribute to high product quality and expertise – a typical strength of German firms. This shows that stakeholder-oriented German firms are likely to profit from their investments in employee relations because attitudes and performance of employees are improved when firms are able to create levels of mutual exchange (Tsui, Pearce, Porter, & Tripoli, 1997).

Additionally, networks and large owners can play an important role in learning and innovation processes. Dyer and Hatch (2006) show, for instance, that carefully maintained networks with important stakeholders enhance knowledge sharing and creation, which finally leads to superior firm performance. Establishing interactions between firms through board interlocks is a typical element of Germany's corporate governance and has positive implications for strategic decisions and learning processes of firms. An example is the impact of board networks on the investment decisions of German firms in the newly accessible countries of Eastern Europe after the fall of the Iron Curtain in 1990 (Tuschke et al., 2014). Interlocks to peers with experience in Eastern European countries helped these firms to learn about the opportunities and risks in these markets and made investments more likely. Although board networks have been shown to provide positive effects also in shareholder-oriented governance system like the U.S., German board interlock networks are different with respect to the density and characteristics of interlocks. For instance, van Veen and Elbertsen (2008) found that German firms, due to the structural arrangements of the German corporate governance system, are less likely to have foreigners on their supervisory boards. Thus, German board networks exist primarily between German companies, leading to dense and unique national networks. At the same time, however, adverse effects associated with the social cohesion and intransparency inherent to these dense networks (Useem, 1984) are reduced by regulation limiting the number of boards an individual is allowed to serve on as well as soft laws calling for diversity (with regard to background, gender, and skills) within boards. Further, compared to market-oriented economies with more dispersed ownership structures, a high number of interlocks between firms in Germany were created based on equity cross-holdings (La Porta et al., 1999; Windolf & Beyer, 1996), thus, coupling personal ties and ownership structures. Similar structures can be found in other stakeholder-oriented systems (Aguilera & Jackson, 2003) and seem to be a correlate of stakeholder-oriented corporate governance. While both, the traditional networks based on interlocks as well as cross-holdings, have diminished – partially due to deliberate efforts to reduce these phenomena, they are still a relevant part of the German governance landscape providing potential benefits for firms.

Another example from the German car manufacturing industry supports this view. The Quandt family has been a major shareholder and an influencing force at BMW – one of the largest German car manufacturing companies – since the 20th century. In 2013, the Quandt family invested in SGL Carbon and Susanne Klatten, a member of the Quandt family, took over the chairman position (Sueddeutsche Zeitung, 2013). SGL Carbon produces carbon fibers that are used to manufacture lightweight automobiles and are expected to be of great importance for future competitiveness in the automotive sector. As investors and owner of the chairman position at SGL Carbon and with a seat and a strong voice at the board of BMW, the Quandt family established a link to spur innovations and organizational learning between these two companies. Thus, providing further evidence for the assumption that unique board characteristics of national governance systems do have direct effects on firm-level behavior (Chang et al., 2015).

Beyond positive effects on innovativeness and learning capabilities, the influence of owners with robust and lasting relations to firms can also work as protection against competitors. Schneper and Guillén (2004), for instance, show that the likelihood of hostile takeover increases when rights of workers and banks are less protected in comparison to shareholder rights. In the case of Roland Berger Strategy Consultants (RBSC), the number three in the German consulting market, internationalization efforts could only be realized without falling victim to hostile takeover attempts due to a strong commitment of RBSC's owners. In 2010, RBSC's limited financial power restricted its ability for expansion in international markets and takeover attempts by multinational accounting firms could only be repelled by a coalition of RBSC's founder and related partners who were willing to invest a substantial part of their capital to finance the firm's further internationalization (Handelsblatt, 2013). Thus, only by the commitment of their cooperative owners, RBSC succeeded in remaining independent. Such an example can also be found in shareholder-oriented governance settings, but is more likely and attainable in a setting that favors cooperative relations between owners and firm management. However, it should be noted that the influence of large owners in Germany is sometimes also associated with decreased flexibility and a limitation of investments. Nevertheless, empirical studies on concentrated ownership in Germany often suggest positive relations with firm performance (Gorton & Schmid, 2000). This applies especially to the case that large blockholders are also part of the founding family (Andres, 2008).

These empirical studies and the example of RBSC also point to a further potential advantage of Germany's stakeholder orientation – the long-term perspective on strategic developments. Different time horizons regarding firm strategy seem to be one of the fundamental discrepancies between shareholder and stakeholder orientation (Aguilera & Jackson, 2003; Yoshikawa & Rasheed, 2009). While firms in shareholder-oriented governance settings are generally under strong pressure from capital markets – which are often short-term focused – stakeholder-oriented governance systems expose a more long-term perspective due to the firm-specific boundedness of stakeholders. Although the long-term existence and prosperity of a company are in the interest of many shareholders, it is not necessarily their primary goal. For shareholders, for instance, who are planning to divest their ownership in a firm, short-term profits are by far more attractive. This can create conflicts between short-term profit motives of some shareholder groups and long-term interests of other stakeholders of a firm. Stakeholder value orientation, in contrast, is expected to lead to a more sustainable and holistic perspective on firm performance and to be less driven by short-term profit maximization (Laplume et al., 2008).

Accordingly, a problem associated with the more sustainable and holistic perspective of Germany's corporate governance is that strategic decisions might be less oriented towards maximizing profits. It is assumed that stakeholder-oriented governance helps influential stakeholder groups to advance individual rents at the expense of the firm (Freeman et al., 2010).

However, a lot of what is regarded as a valuable resource only develops over a longer time. Therefore, managing stakeholder relations in a way that adheres to the needs of a firm as well as its stakeholders in a mutually beneficial manner might increase overall welfare of all parties (Harrison et al., 2010; Walsh, 2005). Following these lines of thought, stakeholder orientation and management in Germany could constitute valuable resources in several ways.

4.6 Towards a Modern Stakeholder Value Approach

It should not be disregarded that a governance system characterized by a strong stakeholder value orientation poses unique challenges and problems. For instance, close relations with various stakeholder groups can be used to disguise a lack of transparency towards capital markets as well as a paucity of control over the firm's management. Many common practices in Anglo-American firms that address exactly these problems were nonexistent in Germany for a long time. Among these practices are large and professionalized investor relations departments, periodic roadshows to meet with important analysts and investors as well as transparent accounting standards. In fact, a lack of transparency and a reluctance to answer the needs of global investors hindered the development of capital markets and created problems with regard to the financial strength of German firms (Hackethal, Schmidt, & Tyrell, 2005). Today, structures and practices that enhance information transparency and market-based control over management are frequently used, as German firms have recognized the importance of access to global capital markets.

Besides increasing information transparency and market-based control over management, lawmakers addressed some challenges of a stakeholder-oriented governance system in a way that is unique to Germany. A change in tax laws, for instance, made it easier for German firms and banks to sell their equity stakes in other firms (Weber, 2009). As a result, the high density of equity cross-holdings between firms could be reduced, thus exposing the firms more to the demands of capital markets. In addition to the decomposition of equity crossholdings, several agencies were founded to supervise firms and to avoid problems such as insider trade, insufficient financial disclosure, or unclear voting rights (Cioffi, 2002), which commonly occur in stakeholder systems because of power imbalance between different stakeholder groups.

An important step in the modernization of Germany's stakeholder systems was the creation of the German Corporate Governance Code (GCGC), which was introduced in 2002 (Jackson & Moerke, 2005). This code of conduct aims at higher transparency and more control from capital markets by integrating selected elements of a shareholder value-oriented governance approach into the existing stakeholder-oriented corporate governance. For instance, it recommends supervisory boards to be more professionalized and to take a more active role in firm governance without recommending to change the general two-tier board structure. To provide orientation and to avoid conflicts, the GCGC tries to find compromises for different stakeholder groups. In doing so, it is well aligned with decision-making processes in typical stakeholder-oriented systems.

It is also argued that the increased orientation towards capital markets as well as the associated stronger engagement of institutional investors are central reasons for Germany's economic recovery over the last few years. Irrespective of a strong stakeholder-orientation, typical shareholder-oriented elements like financial performance indicators and value-based metrics play a major role in the management of German firms. However, in contrast to their U.S. counterparts, German firms do not necessarily view value-based metrics as a strategic goal; rather it is seen as a means of corporate planning and control. By doing this, firms can meet the requirements of global capital markets without affecting the highly valued tradition of stakeholder orientation. In this sense, Germany's corporate governance pursues a modern stakeholder approach that aims at combining positive aspects of "both worlds". Table 5 summarizes the benefits but also the potential problems associated with a stakeholder-oriented corporate governance system that we have discussed so far.

Table 5: Overview of Potential Benefits and Problems of a Stakeholder-oriented Corporate Governance

Potential Benefits:	Potential Problems:
<ul><li>Long-term perspective on value creation & firm performance</li><li>Commitment of stakeholders to firms & strategic decisions</li><li>Greater stability & resilience</li><li>Higher social legitimacy</li><li>Organizational learning & innovation</li><li>Close networks & increased cooperation</li><li>Anticipation of stakeholder needs & reactions</li></ul>	<ul><li>Unresolvable conflicts and higher costs due to concentration on multiple interest groups</li><li>Strategic decisions may be less oriented towards maximizing profits</li><li>Success of stakeholder approach depends on effectiveness of stakeholder management and quality of existing relations</li><li>Lack of transparency towards capital markets</li><li>Paucity of control over the firm's management</li></ul>

4.7 Discussion

In this paper, we examined stakeholder orientation as a central characteristic of the German corporate governance system. We asked whether this orientation is an advantage or disadvantage for German firms regarding their competitiveness in international markets and highlighted positive impacts in areas such as innovations, organizational learning, or change management. Despite the interest in shareholder vs. stakeholder conceptions of corporate governance, their analysis is predominantly conducted with an agency perspective (Jensen, 2002; Jensen & Meckling, 1976) in mind, leading to predisposed support for shareholder conceptions because potential benefits resulting from stakeholder engagement are often neglected.

In our discussion, we demonstrated that a stakeholder-oriented governance system can have a number of advantages. Stable relations with stakeholders based on mutual trust and commitment can create constant access to valuable resources. Moreover, a stronger commitment towards stakeholders may support innovations and organizational learning and may help the firm to manage change. German firms may tap the potential of stakeholder relations more effectively because they are highly experienced in doing so. Refined knowledge and expertise in stakeholder management enable them to understand the value of stakeholder relations. It could be argued that they know how to profit from relations to stakeholders rather than view them as time-consuming and non-effective. Stable relations with stakeholders as well as expertise in stakeholder management are institutionally anchored in the German governance system. This provides an environment in which positive effects of stakeholder management are facilitated.

On the other hand, we have also highlighted some of the potential problems associated with stakeholder-oriented corporate governance such as unresolvable conflicts among stakeholder groups or higher costs. For some of these potential problems, we have discussed how they have been addressed by firms and policy makers in Germany by implementing mechanisms that are more common to shareholder-oriented governance systems. For example, German firms have recognized the importance of access to global capital markets and have therefore installed structures and practices that enhance information transparency and market-based control over management. We have also shown how lawmakers have promoted the decomposition of equity cross-holdings between firms, thus exposing firms more to the demands of capital markets. Additionally, several agencies have been founded to supervise firms better and to avoid problems commonly associated with the imbalance of power between different stakeholders such as insufficient financial disclosure or unclear voting rights.

However, one major problem with the stakeholder approach that remains is that its success depends strongly on the quality of the existing relations. Particularly, strong stakeholder groups that are not managed adequately can diminish rather than enhance firm performance (Coff, 1999). Whereas stakeholder relationships characterized by mutual trust and commitment towards the success of the firm can serve to benefit the firm, relationships which lack these criteria can detract value. In light of recent scandals among German firms (i.e. the bribery scandal at Siemens in 2007, the recent scandal at Volkswagen involving the use of software to circumvent U.S. emissions standards), German firms, regulators, and society at large have highlighted weak, clannish, or self-interested stakeholder relationships as partially responsible. For example, Volkswagen has been described as having a "clannish board" as well as unusually high levels of mutual backscratching among owners, unions, and the government (New York Times, 2015). Although Volkswagen stands out among German firms in its unusual governance hybrid of family control, government ownership, and labor influence, it could be argued that Germany's stakeholder-oriented governance approach may be conducive to scandals when stakeholder interests are highly intertwined. However, instead of generating doubts about the benefits of a stakeholder-oriented corporate governance, these scandals have instead led to an effort to look for ways to improving the quality of relationships with stakeholders. This ongoing discussion in Germany, for example, involves ways in which worker co-determination can help to reduce a climate of performance pressure and intimidation that was said to be conducive to deception and fraud at Volkswagen (Manager Magazin, 2015). Furthermore, in a recent interview, Manfred Getz, chairman of the German Corporate Governance Code Commission, suggested that completely eliminating corporate scandals via corporate governance regulation is impossible. According to Getz, criminal acts will at some point have to be left to legal prosecutors, especially in light of Germany's current mixture of incorporated shareholder value practices and an institutionalized stakeholder-oriented rationale. Instead, he called for all stakeholders to become involved in improving firm culture and values (Die Welt, 2016).

Lessons from the German context portrayed in this essay could serve as blueprint and comparison for adaptations in other corporate governance systems. One the one hand, shareholder systems, for instance, the system of the U.S., could learn from the German model of governance and how German firms are able to manage stakeholder relations in a mutually beneficial manner. One the other hand, stakeholder-oriented systems may also learn from the German approach. For instance, Japan's often cited stakeholder regime suffered from ongoing stagnation over the last decades (Garside, 2012). Supposedly, a too-strong stakeholder orientation could have been a cause for this. Against this background, it seems interesting that German firms adhered to an overall stakeholder orientation while incorporating selected elements of a more shareholder-oriented approach. This allows for a modern stakeholder approach that answers the needs of global capital markets while staying strongly embedded in a stakeholder-oriented governance system. Thus, in the absence of an ideal prototype model of corporate governance (Yoshikawa & Rasheed, 2009), hybrid solutions which intelligently integrate different elements, like it is the case in Germany, could turn out to be successful.

Irrespective of ideological contentions about the relative merits of shareholder or stakeholder orientation and cooperative or competitive approaches to stakeholder relations, corporate governance research should continue to investigate how differences in stakeholder orientation between countries impact firm-level outcomes. Research interested in relative advantages of any governance model should explore how and when different modes of stakeholder relations contribute to firm outcomes to advance our knowledge on the role of governance settings for the competitiveness of firms.

Against this background, it is also important to note that classifications into shareholder or stakeholder governance are not as clear as theory suggests. First, stakeholder orientation can be interpreted differently depending on the national governance context. For U.S. firms settled in a shareholder-oriented governance setting, stakeholder orientation means that firms address other stakeholder groups more than one would normally expect of them. On the contrary, in stakeholder-oriented governance settings, such as Germany, the same amount of stakeholder orientation would not be viewed as a strong sign of stakeholder orientation because of the higher level of overall stakeholder orientation.

Second, firm leaders may not distinguish between shareholder or stakeholder orientation in their management approach as clearly as the different paradigms seem to suggest (Adams et al., 2011). Lorsch and MacIver (1989) show, for instance, that a majority of corporate directors in the U.S. see themselves as more responsible for the long-term interest of several stakeholders than for shareholder concerns only, but often hide their inner values in board discussions to maintain an image of shareholder focus. In this vein, firms within a given corporate governance system might also try to compensate for restrictions and downsides of the national governance conceptualization. Accordingly, the influence of shareholder- or stakeholder-oriented corporate governance systems on firm outcomes is likely to be moderated by the heterogeneity of management and firm-level decisions.

Third, there is more research needed on the impact of different national corporate governance systems on the mechanisms behind firm-level decisions. We know from a number of prior studies that differences between national corporate governance institutions do influence the success of business strategies at the firm-level (Capron & Guillén, 2009; O'Sullivan, 2000). For example, Kacperczyk (2009) shows that an increase in stakeholder orientation following changes in exogenous conditions can be linked to long-term growth in shareholder value suggesting that firm-level decisions can be more or less adequate depending on the relative position of stakeholders in a certain corporate governance system. Furthermore, Schiehll and Martins (2016) provide an extensive summary of cross-national governance literature with regard to firm-level outcomes that highlights numerous influences of national corporate governance systems on firm strategy and performance. A number of studies have also analyzed the relationship between corporate governance and firm-level decisions and performance specifically for the German market (e.g. Andres, 2008; Fauver & Fuerst, 2006; Kaplan, 1997). However, we still lack knowledge on how exactly managers are influenced in their decision-making by corporate governance. In this regard, prior research has argued that corporate governance may be less influential for managerial decisions because firms find ways to overcome restrictions or only adhere to them symbolically. Fiss and Zajac (2004), for instance, show that the introduction of shareholder-oriented practices in German firms partly aimed at merely signaling shareholder orientation to investors and capital markets, while the convention of a stakeholder-oriented management has not changed fundamentally. Future research, therefore, should pay attention to how corporate governance practices are employed by managers to benefit the firm versus when managers attempt to avoid their adoption.

4.8 Conclusion

In our revisit of Germany's corporate governance, we aimed at taking a fresh look at advantages, downsides, and unique challenges of a stakeholder-oriented system. Linked back to theoretical discussions about shareholder and stakeholder value and differences in international corporate governance, we based our investigation on instrumental stakeholder theory and resource-based approaches to stakeholder management. We revealed that a stakeholder-oriented governance setting like Germany could encourage firms to pursue a thoughtfully implemented stakeholder management. By processes of cooperation, trust, information-sharing, and long-term commitment, stakeholders that are effectively managed can contribute to a firm's competitiveness by providing valuable and unique resources. Additionally, paying attention to stakeholders can lead to more balanced decisions that integrate short- and long-term strategic perspectives. Nevertheless, a traditional stakeholder-oriented system – as it was the case in Germany until the mid-90 s – is likely to have some disadvantages, which can limit its competitiveness. Demands of global capital markets made it necessary for German firms to introduce a number of share-holder-oriented governance elements. However, these elements are strongly embedded in a stakeholder-oriented governance system. In its current mixture of incorporated shareholder value practices and an institutionalized stakeholder-oriented rationale, Germany's corporate governance can be considered as a form of an advanced and modern stakeholder value approach.

5 General Conclusion

The three presented studies in this dissertation stressed the importance of an effective collaboration between management and supervisory bodies as well as between these constituencies and relevant stakeholders of the firm (Conger et al., 2001). Against the background that directors are more involved in strategy development processes and that they play an increasingly active role as partners of a firm's top management (Finkelstein & Mooney, 2003; Pugliese et al., 2009), the first study examined antecedents of effective board advisory. Results of this study revealed that individual expertise and the advisory-related abilities of directors play a major role in the overall effectiveness of the board. Further, results indicated that directors of large and complex firms should aim to professionalize the advisory function through the set-up of advisory-oriented committee structures. This study provided implications for research on board effectiveness (Daily et al., 2003; Dalton et al., 1998; Johnson et al., 2013) and the advice and counsel role of boards (Krause et al., 2013; McDonald et al., 2008) as well as for research on director expertise (Khanna et al., 2014; Kor & Sundaramurthy, 2009) and board committees (Bilimoria & Piderit, 1994; Gore et al., 2011).

Subsequently, the second study examined the influence of the relation of CEO and COB characteristics on R&D investment decisions. Based on existing knowledge about the effects of interpersonal differences for strategic decision-making (Carpenter et al., 2004; Kor & Sundaramurthy, 2009), the study developed a theoretical framework that suggested that differences in career backgrounds as well as in socio-personal characteristics between CEOs and COBs foster R&D investments. The study also showed that these effects are moderated by the amount of shared tenure, thus the familiarity between a CEO and a COB. This research advances the literature around CEO duality (Castañer & Kavadis, 2013; Dalton & Dalton, 2010; Finkelstein & D'aveni, 1994; Krause et al., 2014), behavioral perspectives on the effects of interpersonal differences at the top (Cyert & March, 1963; Kor, 2006; Westphal, 1999), and contingency perspectives on governance relations (Karaevli & Zajac, 2013; Zona et al., 2013).

The third and concluding study challenged some of the common beliefs about stakeholder-oriented corporate governance and investigated potential advantages that stem from a more cooperative approach to stakeholder relations using an instrumental stakeholder perspective (Donaldson & Preston, 1995). This study provided an additional and comprehensive perspective to the co-work of top management teams, corporate boards, and important stakeholder groups in the process of value creation for shareholders and stakeholders of the firm. The study provided a background and discussion basis for readers interested in stakeholder theory (Donaldson & Preston, 1995; Freeman et al., 2010), stakeholder management (Harrison et al., 2010; Hillman & Keim, 2001), international corporate governance research (Aguilera & Jackson, 2010; Schiehll & Martins, 2016), and Germany's corporate governance in particular (Fauver & Fuerst, 2006; Jackson & Moerke, 2005). It also highlighted the relevance of the interplay of national institutional environments with industry- and firm-level competitiveness (Griffiths & Zammuto, 2005).

Overall, the presented studies extend knowledge about processes and characteristics of successful collaboration at the top of the firm. The studies contribute to an advancement of knowledge about corporate governance and strategic management largely from a behavioral perspective. Thus, the results pave the way for future research on the internal functioning of corporate boards and TMTs as well as their interrelation with each other and relevant stakeholder groups.

6 References

Adams, J. S. (1965). Inequity in social exchange. In L. Berkowitz (Ed.), *Advances in experimental social psychology* (Vol. 2, pp. 267-299). New York: Academic Press.

Adams, R. B., Hermalin, B. E., & Weisbach, M. S. (2010). The role of boards of directors in corporate governance: A conceptual framework and survey. *Journal of Economic Literature, 48*(1), 58-107.

Adams, R. B., Licht, A. N., & Sagiv, L. (2011). Shareholders and stakeholders: How do directors decide? *Strategic Management Journal, 32*(12), 1331-1355.

Adler, P. S., & Kwon, S.-W. (2002). Social capital: Prospects for a new concept. *Academy of Management Review, 27*(1), 17-40.

Aguilera, R. V., Filatotchev, I., Gospel, H., & Jackson, G. (2008). An organizational approach to comparative corporate governance: Costs, contingencies, and complementarities. *Organization Science, 19*(3), 475-492.

Aguilera, R. V., & Jackson, G. (2003). The cross-national diversity of corporate governance: Dimensions and determinants. *Academy of Management Review, 28*(3), 447-465.

Aguilera, R. V., & Jackson, G. (2010). Comparative and international corporate governance. *Academy of Management Annals, 4*(1), 485-556.

Aguinis, H., & Glavas, A. (2012). What we know and don't know about corporate social responsibility: A review and research agenda. *Journal of Management, 38*(4), 932-968.

Aiken, L. S., & West, S. G. (1991). *Multiple regression: Testing and interpreting interactions.* Newbury Park: Sage.

Alexiev, A. S., Jansen, J. J. P., Van den Bosch, F. A. J., & Volberda, H. W. (2010). Top management team advice seeking and exploratory innovation: The moderating role of TMT heterogeneity. *Journal of Management Studies, 47*(7), 1343-1364.

Allen, F., Carletti, E., & Marquez, R. (2015). Stakeholder governance, competition, and firm value. *Review of Finance, 19*(3), 1315-1346.

Allen, T. J. (1977). *Managing the flow of technology: Technology transfer and the dissemination of technological information within the R&D organization.* Cambridge, MA: MIT Press.

Amason, A. C. (1996). Distinguishing the effects of functional and dysfunctional conflict on strategic decision making: Resolving a paradox for top management teams. *Academy of Management Journal, 39*(1), 123-148.

Amason, A. C., & Schweiger, D. M. (1997). The effects of conflict on strategic decision making effectiveness and organizational performance. In C. K. W. De Dreu & E. Van de Vliert (Eds.), *Using conflict in organizations* (pp. 101-115). London: Sage.

Amason, A. C., Shrader, R. C., & Tompson, G. H. (2006). Newness and novelty: Relating top management team composition to new venture performance. *Journal of Business Venturing, 21*(1), 125-148.

Anand, N., Gardner, H. K., & Morris, T. I. M. (2007). Knowledge-based innovation: Emergence and embedding of new practice areas in management consulting firms. *Academy of Management Journal, 50*(2), 406-428.

Ancona, D. G., & Caldwell, D. F. (1992). Demography and design: Predictors of new product team performance. *Organization Science, 3*(3), 321-341.

Andres, C. (2008). Large shareholders and firm performance—An empirical examination of founding-family ownership. *Journal of Corporate Finance, 14*(4), 431-445.

Arellano, M., & Bond, S. (1991). Some tests of specification for panel data: Monte Carlo evidence and an application to employment equations. *Review of Economic Studies, 58*(2), 277-297.

Argote, L., & Miron-Spektor, E. (2011). Organizational learning: From experience to knowledge. *Organization Science, 22*(5), 1123-1137.

Balkin, D. B., Markman, G. D., & Gomez-Mejia, L. R. (2000). Is CEO pay in high-technology firms related to innovation? *Academy of Management Journal, 43*(6), 1118-1129.

Bandura, A. (1997). *Self-efficacy: The exercise of control.* New York: Freeman.

Bantel, K. A., & Jackson, S. E. (1989). Top management and innovations in banking: Does the composition of the top team make a difference? *Strategic Management Journal, 10*(S1), 107-124.

Barker III, V. L., & Mueller, G. C. (2002). CEO characteristics and firm R&D spending. *Management Science, 48*(6), 782-801.

Barney, J. (1991). Firm resources and sustained competitive advantage. *Journal of Management, 17*(1), 99-120.

Barney, J. B., & Clark, D. N. (2007). *Resource-based theory: Creating and sustaining competitive advantage.* Oxford: Oxford University Press.

Barney, J. B., & Hansen, M. H. (1994). Trustworthiness as a source of competitive advantage. *Strategic Management Journal, 15*(S1), 175-190.

Baysinger, B., & Hoskisson, R. E. (1989). Diversification strategy and R&D intensity in multiproduct firms. *Academy of Management Journal, 32*(2), 310-332.

Baysinger, B., & Hoskisson, R. E. (1990). The composition of boards of directors and strategic control: Effects on corporate strategy. *Academy of Management Review, 15*(1), 72-87.

Baysinger, B. D., Kosnik, R. D., & Turk, T. A. (1991). Effects of board and ownership structure on corporate R&D strategy. *Academy of Management Journal, 34*(1), 205-214.

Berghoff, H. (2006). The end of family business? The Mittelstand and German capitalism in transition, 1949–2000. *Business History Review, 80*(02), 263-295.

Berle, A., & Means, G. (1932). *The modern corporation and private property.* New York: Macmillan.

Berman, S. L., Down, J., & Hill, C. W. L. (2002). Tacit knowledge as a source of competitive advantage in the National Basketball Association. *Academy of Management Journal, 45*(1), 13-31.

Berman, S. L., Wicks, A. C., Kotha, S., & Jones, T. M. (1999). Does stakeholder orientation matter? The relationship between stakeholder management models and firm financial performance. *Academy of Management Journal, 42*(5), 488-506.

Berrone, P., Surroca, J., & Tribó, J. (2007). Corporate ethical identity as a determinant of firm performance: A test of the mediating role of stakeholder satisfaction. *Journal of Business Ethics, 76*(1), 35-53.

Bhagat, C., Hirt, M., & Kehoe, C. (2013). Tapping the strategic potential of boards. *McKinsey Quarterly*, (1), 91-98.

Bilimoria, D., & Piderit, S. K. (1994). Board committee membership: Effects of sex-based bias. *Academy of Management Journal, 37*(6), 1453-1477.

Black, J. A., & Boal, K. B. (1994). Strategic resources: Traits, configurations and paths to sustainable competitive advantage. *Strategic Management Journal, 15*(S2), 131-148.

Boeker, W. (1997). Strategic change: The influence of managerial characteristics and organizational growth. *Academy of Management Journal, 40*(1), 152-170.

Boivie, S., Graffin, S. D., & Pollock, T. G. (2012). Time for me to fly: Predicting director exit at large firms. *Academy of Management Journal, 55*(6), 1334-1359.

Boyd, B. K. (1995). CEO duality and firm performance: A contingency model. *Strategic Management Journal, 16*(4), 301-312.

Boyd, B. K., Haynes, K. T., & Zona, F. (2011). Dimensions of CEO-board relations. *Journal of Management Studies, 48*(8), 1892-1923.

Braiker, H. B., & Kelley, H. H. (1979). Conflict in the development of close relationships. In R. L. Burgess & T. L. Huston (Eds.), *Social exchange in developing relationships* (pp. 135-168). San Diego, CA: Academic Press.

Brickley, J. A., Coles, J. L., & Jarrell, G. (1997). Leadership structure: Separating the CEO and chairman of the board. *Journal of Corporate Finance, 3*(3), 189-220.

Brown, S. L., & Eisenhardt, K. M. (1995). Product development: Past research, present findings, and future directions. *Academy of Management Review, 20*(2), 343-378.

Brush, T. H., Bromiley, P., & Hendrickx, M. (2000). The free cash flow hypothesis for sales growth and firm performance. *Strategic Management Journal, 21*(4), 455-472.

Byrne, D. E. (1971). *The attraction paradigm.* New York: Academic Press.

Cannella, A. A., Park, J.-H., & Lee, H.-U. (2008). Top management team functional background diversity and firm performance: Examining the roles of team member collocation and environmental uncertainty. *Academy of Management Journal, 51*(4), 768-784.

Cappelli, P., Singh, H., Singh, J., & Useem, M. (2010). The India way: Lessons for the U.S. *Academy of Management Perspectives, 24*(2), 6-24.

Capron, L., & Guillén, M. (2009). National corporate governance institutions and post-acquisition target reorganization. *Strategic Management Journal, 30*(8), 803-833.

Carpenter, M. A., Geletkanycz, M. A., & Sanders, W. G. (2004). Upper echelons research revisited: Antecedents, elements, and consequences of top management team composition. *Journal of Management, 30*(6), 749-778.

Carpenter, M. A., Pollock, T. G., & Leary, M. M. (2003). Testing a model of reasoned risk-taking: Governance, the experience of principals and agents, and global strategy in high-technology IPO firms. *Strategic Management Journal, 24*(9), 803-820.

Carpenter, M. A., & Sanders, W. G. (2009). *Strategic management: A dynamic perspective: Concepts and cases*. Upper Saddle River: Prentice Hall.

Carpenter, M. A., Sanders, W. G., & Gregersen, H. B. (2001). Bundling human capital with organizational context: The impact of international assignment experience on multinational firm performance and CEO pay. *Academy of Management Journal, 44*(3), 493-511.

Carpenter, M. A., & Westphal, J. D. (2001). The strategic context of external network ties: Examining the impact of director appointments on board involvement in strategic decision making. *Academy of Management Journal, 44*(4), 639-660.

Castañer, X., & Kavadis, N. (2013). Does good governance prevent bad strategy? A study of corporate governance, financial diversification, and value creation by French corporations, 2000-2006. *Strategic Management Journal, 34*(7), 863-876.

Castanias, R. P., & Helfat, C. E. (2001). The managerial rents model: Theory and empirical analysis. *Journal of Management, 27*(6), 661-678.

Chang, Y. K., Oh, W.-Y., Park, J. H., & Jang, M. G. (2015). Exploring the relationship between board characteristics and CSR: Empirical evidence from Korea. *Journal of Business Ethics*, 1-18.

Chen, H.-L. (2014). Board capital, CEO power and R&D investment in electronics firms. *Corporate Governance: An International Review, 22*(5), 422-436.

Christmann, P., Day, D., & Yip, G. S. (2000). The relative influence of country conditions, industry structure, and business strategy on multinational corporation subsidiary performance. *Journal of International Management, 5*(4), 241-265.

Cioffi, J. W. (2002). Restructuring "Germany Inc.": The politics of company and takeover law reform in Germany and the European Union. *Law & Policy, 24*(4), 355-402.

Coff, R. W. (1999). When competitive advantage doesn't lead to performance: The resource-based view and stakeholder bargaining power. *Organization Science, 10*(2), 119-133.

Cohen, W. M., & Levinthal, D. A. (1990). Absorptive capacity: A new perspective on learning and innovation. *Administrative Science Quarterly*, 128-152.

Colbert, B. A. (2004). The complex resource-based view: Implications for theory and practice in strategic human resource management. *Academy of Management Review, 29*(3), 341-358.

Conger, J. A., Lawler III, E. E., & Finegold, D. (2001). *Corporate boards: New strategies for adding value at the top*. San Francisco: Jossey-Bass/Wiley.

Crossland, C., & Hambrick, D. C. (2007). How national systems differ in their constraints on corporate executives: A study of CEO effects in three countries. *Strategic Management Journal, 28*(8), 767-789.

Crossland, C., Zyung, J. Y., Hiller, N. J., & Hambrick, D. C. (2014). CEO career variety: Effects on firm-level strategic and social novelty. *Academy of Management Journal, 57*(3), 652-674.

Culpepper, P. D. (1999). The future of the high-skill equilibrium in Germany. *Oxford Review of Economic Policy, 15*(1), 43-59.

Cyert, R. M., & March, J. G. (1963). *A behavioral theory of the firm.* Englewood Cliffs, NJ: Prentice Hall.

Dacin, M. T., Goodstein, J., & Scott, W. R. (2002). Institutional theory and institutional change: Introduction to the special research forum. *Academy of Management Journal, 45*(1), 45-56.

Daily, C. M. (1996). Governance patterns in bankruptcy reorganizations. *Strategic Management Journal, 17*(5), 355-375.

Daily, C. M., & Dalton, D. R. (1992). The relationship between governance structure and corporate performance in entrepreneurial firms. *Journal of Business Venturing, 7*(5), 375-386.

Daily, C. M., Dalton, D. R., & Cannella, A. A. (2003). Corporate governance: Decades of dialogue and data. *Academy of Management Review, 28*(3), 371-382.

Daily, C. M., & Schwenk, C. (1996). Chief executive officers, top management teams, and boards of directors: Congruent or countervailing forces? *Journal of Management, 22*(2), 185-208.

Dalton, D. R., Daily, C. M., Ellstrand, A. E., & Johnson, J. L. (1998). Meta-analytic reviews of board composition, leadership structure, and financial performance. *Strategic Management Journal, 19*(3), 269-290.

Dalton, D. R., & Dalton, C. M. (2010). Integration of micro and macro studies in governance research: CEO duality, board composition, and financial performance. *Journal of Management, 37*(2), 404-411.

Damanpour, F. (2010). An integration of research findings of effects of firm size and market competition on product and process innovations. *British Journal of Management, 21*(4), 996-1010.

David, P., O'Brien, J. P., Yoshikawa, T., & Delios, A. (2010). Do shareholders or stakeholders appropriate the rents from corporate diversification? The influence of ownership structure. *Academy of Management Journal, 53*(3), 636-654.

Dawson, J. F. (2014). Moderation in management research: What, why, when, and how. *Journal of Business and Psychology, 29*(1), 1-19.

De Clercq, D., Thongpapanl, N., & Dimov, D. (2009). When good conflict gets better and bad conflict becomes worse: The role of social capital in the conflict-innovation relationship. *Journal of the Academy of Marketing Science, 37*(3), 283-297.

de Wit, F. R., Greer, L. L., & Jehn, K. A. (2012). The paradox of intragroup conflict: A meta-analysis. *Journal of Applied Psychology, 97*(2), 360-390.

Der Spiegel. (2009). GM Europe: Opelaner billigen Gehaltsverzicht. [Cited 8 August 2014.] Available from URL: http://www.spiegel.de/wirtschaft/unternehmen/gm-europe-opelaner-billigen-gehaltsverzicht-a-658980.html

Deutsch, Y. (2005). The impact of board composition on firms' critical decisions: A meta-analytic review. *Journal of Management, 31*(3), 424-444.

Dezsö, C. L., & Ross, D. G. (2012). Does female representation in top management improve firm performance? A panel data investigation. *Strategic Management Journal, 33*(9), 1072-1089.

Die Welt. (2016). Das bild des ehrbaren kaufmanns ist angekratzt. [Cited 26 June 2016.] Available from URL: http://www.welt.de/wirtschaft/article152231730/Das-Bild-des-ehrbaren-Kaufmanns-ist-angekratzt.html.

Dodd, E. (1932). For whom are corporate managers trustees. *Harvard Law Review, 45*, 1145-1163.

Donaldson, T., & Preston, L. E. (1995). The stakeholder theory of the corporation: Concepts, evidence, and implications. *Academy of Management Review, 20*(1), 65-91.

Downing, J. W., Judd, C. M., & Brauer, M. (1992). Effects of repeated expressions on attitude extremity. *Journal of Personality and Social Psychology, 63*(1), 17-29.

Dyer, J. H., & Hatch, N. W. (2006). Relation-specific capabilities and barriers to knowledge transfers: Creating advantage through network relationships. *Strategic Management Journal, 27*(8), 701-719.

Eisenhardt, K. M. (1989). Making fast strategic decisions in high-velocity environments. *Academy of Management Journal, 32*(3), 543-576.

Empson, L., Muzio, D., & Broschak, J. (2015). *Oxford handbook of professional service firms*. USA: Oxford University Press.

Ericsson, K. A., & Charness, N. (1994). Expert performance: Its structure and acquisition. *American Psychologist, 49*(8), 725-747.

European Parliament. (2012). Relations between company supervisory bodies and the management. [Cited 3 July 2016.] Available from URL: http://www.europarl.europa.eu/thinktank/de/document.html?reference=IPOL-JU-RI_ET(2012)462454

Fama, E. F., & Jensen, M. C. (1983). Separation of ownership and control. *Journal of Law and Economics, 26*(2), 301-325.

Fauver, L., & Fuerst, M. E. (2006). Does good corporate governance include employee representation? Evidence from German corporate boards. *Journal of Financial Economics, 82*(3), 673-710.

Finkelstein, S., & D'aveni, R. A. (1994). CEO duality as a double-edged sword: How boards of directors balance entrenchment avoidance and unity of command. *Academy of Management Journal, 37*(5), 1079-1108.

Finkelstein, S., Hambrick, D. C., & Cannella, A. A. (2009). *Strategic leadership: Theory and research on executives, top management teams, and boards*. Oxford: Oxford University Press.

Finkelstein, S., & Mooney, A. C. (2003). Not the usual suspects: How to use board process to make boards better. *Academy of Management Executive, 17*(2), 101-113.

Fisher, R. (2012). *The social psychology of intergroup and international conflict resolution*. New York: Springer Science & Business Media.

Fiss, P. C., & Zajac, E. J. (2004). The diffusion of ideas over contested terrain: The (non)adoption of a shareholder value orientation among German firms. *Administrative Science Quarterly, 49*(4), 501-534.

Fohlin, C. (2005). The history of corporate ownership and control in germany. In R. K. Morck (Ed.), *A history of corporate governance around the world: Family business groups to professional managers* (pp. 223-282). Chicago: University of Chicago Press.

Forbes, D. P., & Milliken, F. J. (1999). Cognition and corporate governance: Understanding boards of directors as strategic decision-making groups. *Academy of Management Review, 24*(3), 489-505.

Fosstenløkken, S. M., Løwendahl, B. R., & Revang, O. (2003). Knowledge development through client interaction: A comparative study. *Organization Studies, 24*(6), 859-879.

Freeman, R. E. (1984). *Strategic management: A stakeholder approach.* Boston: Pitman.

Freeman, R. E., Harrison, J. S., Wicks, A. C., Parmar, B. L., & De Colle, S. (2010). *Stakeholder theory: The state of the art.* Cambridge: Cambridge University Press.

Freeman, R. E., Wicks, A. C., & Parmar, B. (2004). Stakeholder theory and "the corporate objective revisited". *Organization Science, 15*(3), 364-369.

Friedman, M. (1970, September 13). The social responsibility of business is to increase its profits. *The New York Times Magazine,* pp. 122-126.

Gardner, H. K., Gino, F., & Staats, B. R. (2012). Dynamically integrating knowledge in teams: Transforming resources into performance. *Academy of Management Journal, 55*(4), 998-1022.

Garside, W. R. (2012). *Japan's great stagnation: Forging ahead, falling behind.* Cheltenham: Edward Elgar Publishing.

Gary, M. S., Wood, R. E., & Pillinger, T. (2012). Enhancing mental models, analogical transfer, and performance in strategic decision making. *Strategic Management Journal, 33*(11), 1229-1246.

Glückler, J., & Armbrüster, T. (2003). Bridging uncertainty in management consulting: The mechanisms of trust and networked reputation. *Organization Studies, 24*(2), 269-297.

Godfrey, P. C. (2005). The relationship between corporate philanthropy and shareholder wealth: A risk management perspective. *Academy of Management Review, 30*(4), 777-798.

Golden, B. R., & Zajac, E. J. (2001). When will boards influence strategy? Inclination x power = strategic change. *Strategic Management Journal, 22*(12), 1087-1111.

Gomez-Mejia, L. R., Cruz, C., Berrone, P., & De Castro, J. (2011). The bind that ties: Socioemotional wealth preservation in family firms. *Academy of Management Annals, 5*(1), 653-707.

Goodstein, J., Gautam, K., & Boeker, W. (1994). The effects of board size and diversity on strategic change. *Strategic Management Journal, 15*(3), 241-250.

Gore, A. K., Matsunaga, S., & Eric Yeung, P. (2011). The role of technical expertise in firm governance structure: Evidence from chief financial officer contractual incentives. *Strategic Management Journal, 32*(7), 771-786.

Gorton, G., & Schmid, F. A. (2000). Universal banking and the performance of German firms. *Journal of Financial Economics, 58*(1–2), 29-80.

Gorton, G., & Schmid, F. A. (2004). Capital, labor, and the firm: A study of German codetermination. *Journal of the European Economic Association, 2*(5), 863-905.

Governance Commission. (2015). German corporate governance code. [Cited 03 July 2016.] Available from URL: http://www.dcgk.de//files/dcgk/usercontent/en/download/code/2015-05-05_Corporate_Governance_Code_EN.pdf

Grant, R. M. (1996). Toward a knowledge-based theory of the firm. *Strategic Management Journal, 17*(S2), 109-122.

Graves, S. B., & Langowitz, N. S. (1993). Innovative productivity and returns to scale in the pharmaceutical industry. *Strategic Management Journal, 14*(8), 593-605.

Greene, W. H. (2000). *Econometric analysis* (4th ed.). Upper Saddle River, NJ: Prentice Hall.

Greenwood, R., Li, S. X., Prakash, R., & Deephouse, D. L. (2005). Reputation, diversification, and organizational explanations of performance in professional service firms. *Organization Science, 16*(6), 661-673.

Greve, H. R. (2003). *Organizational learning from performance feedback: A behavioral perspective on innovation and change.* Cambridge, U.K.: Cambridge University Press.

Griffiths, A., & Zammuto, R. F. (2005). Institutional governance systems and variations in national competitive advantage: An integrative framework. *Academy of Management Review, 30*(4), 823-842.

Guthrie, J. P., & Datta, D. K. (1997). Contextual influences on executive selection: Firm characteristics and CEO experience. *Journal of Management Studies, 34*(4), 537-560.

Haas, M. R., & Hansen, M. T. (2005). When using knowledge can hurt performance: The value of organizational capabilities in a management consulting company. *Strategic Management Journal, 26*(1), 1-24.

Hackethal, A., Schmidt, R. H., & Tyrell, M. (2005). Banks and German corporate governance: On the way to a capital market-based system? *Corporate Governance: An International Review, 13*(3), 397-407.

Hackman, J. (1992). Group influences on individuals in organizations. In M. Dunnette & L. Hough (Eds.), *Handbook of industrial and organizational psychology* (Vol. 3, pp. 199-267). Palo Alto, CA: Consulting Psychologists Press.

Hall, P. A., & Soskice, D. (2001). *Varieties of capitalism: The institutional foundations of comparative advantage.* Oxford: Oxford University Press.

Hambrick, D. C. (2007). Upper echelons theory: An update. *Academy of Management Review, 32*(2), 334-343.

Hambrick, D. C., Cho, T. S., & Ming-Jer, C. (1996). The influence of top management team heterogeneity on firms' competitive moves. *Administrative Science Quarterly, 41*(4), 659-684.

Hambrick, D. C., & Mason, P. A. (1984). Upper echelons: The organization as a reflection of its top managers. *The Academy of Management Review, 9*(2), 193-206.

Hambrick, D. C., Werder, A. v., & Zajac, E. J. (2008). New directions in corporate governance research. *Organization Science, 19*(3), 381-385.

Handelsblatt. (2008). GM vor der Insolvenz - Vorschlaege fuer Opel. [Cited 8 August 2014.] Available from URL: http://www.handelsblatt.com/unternehmen/industrie/gescheitertes-rettungspaket-gm-vor-der-insolvenz-vorschlaege-fuer-opel/3071892.html

Handelsblatt. (2013). Roland Berger soll jetzt doch eigenstaendig bleiben. [Cited 8 August 2014.] Available from URL: http://www.handelsblatt.com/unternehmen/handel-dienstleister/kein-verkauf-roland-berger-soll-jetzt-doch-eigenstaendig-bleiben/9228988.html

Hansen, L. P. (1982). Large sample properties of generalized method of moments estimators. *Econometrica, 50*, 1029-1054.

Hansmann, H., & Kraakman, R. (2000). End of history for corporate law. *Georgetown Law Journal, 89*, 439-468.

Harris, D., & Helfat, C. (1997). Specificity of CEO human capital and compensation. *Strategic Management Journal, 18*(11), 895-920.

Harrison, D. A., Price, K. H., & Bell, M. P. (1998). Beyond relational demography: Time and the effects of surface-and deep-level diversity on work group cohesion. *Academy of Management Journal, 41*(1), 96-107.

Harrison, J. R. (1987). The strategic use of corporate board committees. *California Management Review, 30*(1), 109-125.

Harrison, J. S., Bosse, D. A., & Phillips, R. A. (2010). Managing for stakeholders, stakeholder utility functions, and competitive advantage. *Strategic Management Journal, 31*(1), 58-74.

Harrison, J. S., & Wicks, A. C. (2013). Stakeholder theory, value, and firm performance. *Business Ethics Quarterly, 23*(1), 97-124.

Hausman, J. A. (1978). Specification tests in econometrics. *Econometrica: Journal of the Econometric Society*, 1251-1271.

Haynes, K. T., & Hillman, A. (2010). The effect of board capital and CEO power on strategic change. *Strategic Management Journal, 31*(11), 1145-1163.

He, J., & Huang, Z. (2011). Board informal hierarchy and firm financial performance: Exploring a tacit structure guiding boardroom interactions. *Academy of Management Journal, 54*(6), 1119-1139.

Heinze, T. (2004). Dynamics in the German system of corporate governance? Empirical findings regarding interlocking directorates. *Economy & Society, 33*(2), 218-238.

Henke, J. W. (1986). Involving the board of directors in strategic planning. *Journal of Business Strategy, 7*(2), 87-95.

Heugens, P., van den Bosch, F., & van Riel, C. (2002). Stakeholder integration building mutually enforcing relationships. *Business & Society, 41*(1), 36-60.

Hillman, A. J., Cannella, J. A. A., & Paetzold, R. L. (2000). The resource dependence role of corporate directors: Strategic adaptation of board composition in response to environmental change. *Journal of Management Studies, 37*(2), 235-255.

Hillman, A. J., & Dalziel, T. (2003). Boards of directors and firm performance: Integrating agency and resource dependence perspectives. *Academy of Management Review, 28*(3), 383-396.

Hillman, A. J., & Keim, G. D. (2001). Shareholder value, stakeholder management, and social issues: What's the bottom line? *Strategic Management Journal, 22*(2), 125-139.

Hillman, A. J., Shropshire, C., Certo, S. T., Dalton, D. R., & Dalton, C. M. (2010). What I like about you: A multilevel study of shareholder discontent with director monitoring. *Organization Science, 22*(3), 675-687.

Hitt, M. A., Bierman, L., Uhlenbruck, K., & Shimizu, K. (2006). The importance of resources in the internationalization of professional service firms: The good, the bad, and the ugly. *Academy of Management Journal, 49*(6), 1137-1157.

Hitt, M. A., Biermant, L., Shimizu, K., & Kochhar, R. (2001). Direct and moderating effects of human capital on strategy and performance in professional service firms: A resource-based perspective. *Academy of Management Journal, 44*(1), 13-28.

Hitt, M. A., Hoskisson, R. E., & Kim, H. (1997). International diversification: Effects on innovation and firm performance in product-diversified firms. *Academy of Management Journal, 40*(4), 767-798.

Hosmer, L. T., & Kiewitz, C. (2005). Organizational justice: A behavioral science concept with critical implications for business ethics and stakeholder theory. *Business Ethics Quarterly, 15*(1), 67-91.

Huckman, R. S., Staats, B. R., & Upton, D. M. (2009). Team familiarity, role experience, and performance: Evidence from Indian software services. *Management Science, 55*(1), 85-100.

Hutchinson, R. W. (1995). The capital structure and investment decisions of the small owner-managed firm: Some exploratory issues. *Small Business Economics, 7*(3), 231-239.

Jackson, G. (2001). The origins of nonliberal corporate governance in Germany and Japan. In W. Streeck, & Yamamura, K. (Ed.), *The origins of nonliberal capitalism: Germany and Japan compared* (pp. 121-170). Ithaca, NY: Cornell University Press.

Jackson, G., & Moerke, A. (2005). Continuity and change in corporate governance: Comparing Germany and Japan. *Corporate Governance: An International Review, 13*(3), 351-361.

James, H. S. (1999). Owner as manager, extended horizons and the family firm. *International Journal of the Economics of Business, 6*(1), 41-55.

Jehn, K. A. (1995). A multimethod examination of the benefits and detriments of intragroup conflict. *Administrative Science Quarterly, 40*(2), 256-282.

Jehn, K. A. (1997). A qualitative analysis of conflict types and dimensions in organizational groups. *Administrative Science Quarterly, 42*(3), 530-557.

Jehn, K. A., & Mannix, E. A. (2001). The dynamic nature of conflict: A longitudinal study of intragroup conflict and group performance. *Academy of Management Journal, 44*(2), 238-251.

Jensen, M., & Zajac, E. J. (2004). Corporate elites and corporate strategy: How demographic preferences and structural position shape the scope of the firm. *Strategic Management Journal, 25*(6), 507-524.

Jensen, M. C. (2002). Value maximization, stakeholder theory, and the corporate objective function. *Business Ethics Quarterly, 12*(2), 235-256.

Jensen, M. C., & Meckling, W. H. (1976). Theory of the firm: Managerial behavior, agency costs and ownership structure. *Journal of Financial Economics, 3*(4), 305-360.

Jensen, M. C., & Murphy, K. J. (1990). Performance pay and top-management incentives. *Journal of Political Economy*, 225-264.

Jiao, Y. (2010). Stakeholder welfare and firm value. *Journal of Banking & Finance, 34*(10), 2549-2561.

Johnson, J. L., Ellstrand, A. E., & Daily, C. M. (1996). Boards of directors: A review and research agenda. *Journal of Management, 22*(3), 409-438.

Johnson, S. G., Schnatterly, K., & Hill, A. D. (2013). Board composition beyond independence social capital, human capital, and demographics. *Journal of Management, 39*(1), 232-262.

Jones, T. M. (1995). Instrumental stakeholder theory: A synthesis of ethics and economics. *Academy of Management Review, 20*(2), 404-437.

Judge, W. Q., & Zeithaml, C. P. (1992). Institutional and strategic choice perspectives on board involvement in the strategic decision process. *Academy of Management Journal, 35*(4), 766-794.

Jürgens, U., Naumann, K., & Rupp, J. (2000). Shareholder value in an adverse environment: The German case. *Economy & Society, 29*(1), 54-79.

Kacperczyk, A. (2009). With greater power comes greater responsibility? Takeover protection and corporate attention to stakeholders. *Strategic Management Journal, 30*(3), 261-285.

Kaczmarek, S., Kimino, S., & Pye, A. (2012). Antecedents of board composition: The role of nomination committees. *Corporate Governance: An International Review, 20*(5), 474-489.

Kakabadse, A. P., Kakabadse, N. K., & Knyght, R. (2010). The chemistry factor in the chairman/CEO relationship. *European Management Journal, 28*(4), 285-296.

Kaplan, S. N. (1997). Corporate governance and corporate performance: A comparison of Germany, Japan, and the US. *Journal of Applied Corporate Finance, 9*(4), 86-93.

Kaplan, S. N., & Minton, B. A. (2012). How has CEO turnover changed? *International Review of Finance, 12*(1), 57-87.

Karaevli, A. (2007). Performance consequences of new CEO 'Outsiderness': Moderating effects of pre- and post-succession contexts. *Strategic Management Journal, 28*(7), 681-706.

Karaevli, A., & Zajac, E. J. (2013). When do outsider CEOs generate strategic change? The enabling role of corporate stability. *Journal of Management Studies, 50*(7), 1267-1294.

Kassin, S. (2003). *Psychology*. USA: Prantice-Hall, Inc.

Kesner, I. F. (1988). Directors' characteristics and committee membership: An investigation of type, occupation, tenure, and gender. *Academy of Management Journal, 31*(1), 66-84.

Khanna, P., Jones, C. D., & Boivie, S. (2014). Director human capital, information processing demands, and board effectiveness. *Journal of Management, 40*(2), 557-585.

Khanna, T., Kogan, J., & Palepu, K. (2006). Globalization and similarities in corporate governance: A cross-country analysis. *Review of Economics & Statistics, 88*(1), 69-90.

Kim, C., & Bettis, R. A. (2014). Cash is surprisingly valuable as a strategic asset. *Strategic Management Journal, 35*(13), 2053-2063.

Klarner, P., Sarstedt, M., Hoeck, M., & Ringle, C. M. (2013). Disentangling the effects of team competences, team adaptability, and client communication on the performance of management consulting teams. *Long Range Planning, 46*(3), 258-286.

Klingebiel, R., & Rammer, C. (2014). Resource allocation strategy for innovation portfolio management. *Strategic Management Journal, 35*(2), 246-268.

Kogut, B., & Zander, U. (1993). Knowledge of the firm and the evolutionary theory of the multinational corporation. *Journal of International Business Studies, 24*(4), 625-645.

Kor, Y. Y. (2003). Experience-based top management team competence and sustained growth. *Organization Science, 14*(6), 707-719.

Kor, Y. Y. (2006). Direct and interaction effects of top management team and board compositions on R&D investment strategy. *Strategic Management Journal, 27*(11), 1081-1099.

Kor, Y. Y., & Misangyi, V. F. (2008). Outside directors' industry-specific experience and firms' liability of newness. *Strategic Management Journal, 29*(12), 1345-1355.

Kor, Y. Y., & Sundaramurthy, C. (2009). Experience-based human capital and social capital of outside directors. *Journal of Management, 35*(4), 981-1006.

Korsgaard, M. A., Schweiger, D. M., & Sapienza, H. J. (1995). Building commitment, attachment, and trust in strategic decision-making teams: The role of procedural justice. *Academy of Management Journal, 38*(1), 60-84.

Kotter, J. P., & Cohen, D. S. (2002). *The heart of change.* Boston: Harvard Business School Press.

Krause, R., Semadeni, M., & Cannella, A. A. (2013). External COO/presidents as expert directors: A new look at the service role of boards. *Strategic Management Journal, 34*(13), 1628-1641.

Krause, R., Semadeni, M., & Cannella, A. A. (2014). CEO duality: A review and research agenda. *Journal of Management, 40*(1), 256-286.

Kroll, M., Walters, B. A., & Le, S. A. (2007). The impact of board composition and top management team ownership structure on post-IPO performance in young entrepreneurial firms. *Academy of Management Journal, 50*(5), 1198-1216.

Kroll, M., Walters, B. A., & Wright, P. (2008). Board vigilance, director experience, and corporate outcomes. *Strategic Management Journal, 29*(4), 363-382.

Kutner, M., Nachtsheim, C., & Neter, J. (2004). *Applied linear regression models* (4th ed.). New York: McGraw-Hill Irwin.

La Porta, R., Lopez-de-Silanes, F., & Shleifer, A. (1999). Corporate ownership around the world. *Journal of Finance, 54*(2), 471-517.

Laplume, A. O., Sonpar, K., & Litz, R. A. (2008). Stakeholder theory: Reviewing a theory that moves us. *Journal of Management, 34*(6), 1152-1189.

Lee, M.-D. P. (2008). A review of the theories of corporate social responsibility: Its evolutionary path and the road ahead. *International Journal of Management Reviews, 10*(1), 53-73.

Lewin, A. Y., Massini, S., & Carine, P. (2011). Microfoundations of internal and external absorptive capacity routines. *Organization Science, 22*(1), 81-98.

Liebeskind, J. P. (1996). Knowledge, strategy, and the theory of the firm. *Strategic Management Journal, 17*(S2), 93-107.

Lines, R. (2004). Influence of participation in strategic change: Resistance, organizational commitment and change goal achievement. *Journal of Change Management, 4*(3), 193-215.

Littlepage, G., Robison, W., & Reddington, K. (1997). Effects of task experience and group experience on group performance, member ability, and recognition of expertise. *Organizational Behavior and Human Decision Processes, 69*(2), 133-147.

Lorsch, J., & MacIver, E. (1989). *Pawns or potentates: The reality of America's corporate boards, 1989*. Boston: Harvard Business School Press.

Lublin, J. (2012, June 6). More CEOs sharing control at the top. *Wall Street Journal,* B1.

Manager Magazin. (2015). Warum die interne Kontrolle bei VW erneut versagt hat. [Cited 26 June 2016.] Available from URL: http://www.managermagazin.de/unternehmen/autoindustrie/zwei-gruende-warum-die-interne-kontrolle-bei-vw-erneut-versagt-hat-a-1054967.html.

Margolis, J. D., & Walsh, J. P. (2003). Misery loves companies: Rethinking social initiatives by business. *Administrative Science Quarterly, 48*(2), 268-305.

McDonald, M. L., & Westphal, J. D. (2003). Getting by with the advice of their friends: CEOs' advice networks and firms' strategic responses to poor performance. *Administrative Science Quarterly, 48*(1), 1-32.

McDonald, M. L., Westphal, J. D., & Graebner, M. E. (2008). What do they know? The effects of outside director acquisition experience on firm acquisition performance. *Strategic Management Journal, 29*(11), 1155-1177.

McNulty, T., & Pettigrew, A. (1999). Strategists on the board. *Organization Studies, 20*(1), 47-74.

Menon, A., Bharadwaj, S. G., & Howell, R. (1996). The quality and effectiveness of marketing strategy: Effects of functional and dysfunctional conflict in intraorganizational relationships. *Journal of the Academy of Marketing Science, 24*(4), 299-313.

Michel, J. G., & Hambrick, D. C. (1992). Diversification posture and top management team characteristics. *Academy of Management Journal, 35*(1), 9-37.

Morck, R., Shleifer, A., & Vishny, R. W. (1989). Alternative mechanisms for corporate control. *The American Economic Review, 79*(4), 842-852.

Mueller, S. (2012). Works councils and establishment productivity. *Industrial & Labor Relations Review, 65*(4), 880-898.

Nadler, D. A. (2004). Building better boards. *Harvard Business Review, 82*(5), 102-111.

Nadolska, A., & Barkema, H. G. (2014). Good learners: How top management teams affect the success and frequency of acquisitions. *Strategic Management Journal, 35*(10), 1483-1507.

Naranjo-Gil, D., Hartmann, F., & Maas, V. S. (2008). Top management team heterogeneity, strategic change and operational performance. *British Journal of Management, 19*(3), 222-234.

Ndofor, H. A., Sirmon, D. G., & He, X. (2015). Utilizing the firm's resources: How TMT heterogeneity and resulting faultlines affect TMT tasks. *Strategic Management Journal, 36*(11), 1656-1674.

New York Times. (2015). Problems at Volkswagen start in the boardroom. [Cited 26 June 2016.] Available from URL: http://www.nytimes.com/2015/09/25/business/international/problems-at-volkswagen-start-in-the-boardroom.html?_r=0.

Nonaka, I., & von Krogh, G. (2009). Perspective-tacit knowledge and knowledge conversion: Controversy and advancement in organizational knowledge creation theory. *Organization Science, 20*(3), 635-652.

Novick, L. R. (1988). Analogical transfer, problem similarity, and expertise. *Journal of Experimental Psychology: Learning, Memory, and Cognition, 14*(3), 510-520.

O'Sullivan, M. (2000). Corporate governance and globalization. *The Annals of the American Academy of Political and Social Science, 570*(1), 153-172.

Ogden, S., & Watson, R. (1999). Corporate performance and stakeholder management: Balancing shareholder and customer interests in the UK privatized water industry. *Academy of Management Journal, 42*(5), 526-538.

Oliver, C. (1992). The antecedents of deinstitutionalization. *Organization Studies, 13*(4), 563-588.

Parker, H. (1990). The company chairman - his role and responsibilities. *Long Range Planning, 23*(4), 35-43.

Phillips, R., Freeman, R. E., & Wicks, A. C. (2003). What stakeholder theory is not. *Business Ethics Quarterly, 13*(4), 479-502.

Ployhart, R. E., & Moliterno, T. P. (2011). Emergence of the human capital resource: A multilevel model. *Academy of Management Review, 36*(1), 127-150.

Pugliese, A., Bezemer, P.-J., Zattoni, A., Huse, M., Van den Bosch, F. A. J., & Volberda, H. W. (2009). Boards of directors' contribution to strategy: A literature review and research agenda. *Corporate Governance: An International Review, 17*(3), 292-306.

Quigley, T. J., & Hambrick, D. C. (2012). When the former ceo stays on as board chair: effects on successor discretion, strategic change, and performance. *Strategic Management Journal, 33*(7), 834-859.

Rindova, V. P. (1999). What corporate boards have to do with strategy: A cognitive perspective. *Journal of Management Studies, 36*(7), 953-975.

Roberts, J. (2002). Building the complementary board. The work of the plc chairman. *Long Range Planning, 35*(5), 493-520.

Roberts, J., & Stiles, P. (1999). The relationship between chairmen and chief executives: Competitive or complementary roles? *Long Range Planning, 32*(1), 36-48.

Roquebert, J. A., Phillips, R. L., & Westfall, P. A. (1996). Markets vs. management: What 'drives' profitability? *Strategic Management Journal, 17*(8), 653-664.

Rousseeuw, P. J., & Leroy, A. M. (2005). *Robust regression and outlier detection.* New York: John Wiley & Sons.

Rumelt, R., Schendel, D., & Teece, D. (1994). *Fundamental issues in strategy.* Boston, MA: Harvard Business School Press.

Sanders, W. G., & Tuschke, A. (2007). The adoption of institutionally contested organizational practices: The emergence of stock option pay in Germany. *Academy of Management Journal, 50*(1), 33-56.

Schaubroeck, J., & Lam, S. S. (2002). How similarity to peers and supervisor influences organizational advancement in different cultures. *Academy of Management Journal, 45*(6), 1120-1136.

Schiehll, E., & Martins, H. C. (2016). Cross-national governance research: A systematic review and assessment. *Corporate Governance: An International Review, 24*(3), 181-199.

Schneper, W. D., & Guillén, M. F. (2004). Stakeholder rights and corporate governance: A cross-national study of hostile takeovers. *Administrative Science Quarterly, 49*(2), 263-295.

Schweiger, D. M., Sandberg, W. R., & Ragan, J. W. (1986). Group approaches for improving strategic decision making: A comparative analysis of dialectical inquiry, devil's advocacy, and consensus. *Academy of Management Journal, 29*(1), 51-71.

Schweiger, D. M., Sandberg, W. R., & Rechner, P. L. (1989). Experiential effects of dialectical inquiry, devil's advocacy and consensus approaches to strategic decision making. *Academy of Management Journal, 32*(4), 745-772.

Shen, W. (2003). The dynamics of the CEO-board relationship: An evolutionary perspective. *Academy of Management Review, 28*(3), 466-476.

Shen, W., & Cannella, A. A. (2002). Revisiting the performance consequences of CEO succession: The impacts of successor type, postsuccession senior executive turnover, and departing CEO tenure. *Academy of Management Journal, 45*(4), 717-733.

Shen, W., & Cannella, A. A. (2003). Will succession planning increase shareholder wealth? Evidence from investor reactions to relay CEO successions. *Strategic Management Journal, 24*(2), 191-198.

Shleifer, A., & Vishny, R. W. (1997). A survey of corporate governance. *Journal of Finance, 52*(2), 737-783.

Singh, R., & Ho, S. Y. (2000). Attitudes and attraction: A new test of the attraction, repulsion and similarity-dissimilarity asymmetry hypotheses. *British Journal of Social Psychology, 39*(2), 197-211.

SpencerStuart. (2015). *Spencer Stuart board index.* Chicago.

Sternberg, R. J. (1997). *Successful intelligence.* New York, NY: Penguin Putnam.

Sueddeutsche Zeitung. (2013). Klatten wird Aufsichtsratchefin von SGL Carbon. [Cited 8 August 2014.] Available from URL: http://www.sueddeutsche.de/wirtschaft/quandt-erbin-klatten-wird-aufsichtsratchefin-von-sgl-carbon-1.1662313

Sundaramurthy, C., & Lewis, M. (2003). Control and collaboration: Paradoxes of governance. *Academy of Management Review, 28*(3), 397-415.

Surroca, J., & Tribó, J. A. (2008). Managerial entrenchment and corporate social performance. *Journal of Business Finance & Accounting, 35*(5-6), 748-789.

Tagesschau. (2011). Auferstanden nach der Krise. [Cited 14 January 2016.] Available from URL: https://www.tagesschau.de/wirtschaft/automobilstandort102.html

Tajfel, H., & Turner, J. C. (2004). The social identity theory of intergroup behavior. In J. T. Jost & J. Sidanius (Eds.), *Political psychology* (pp. 276–293). New York: Psychology Press.

Teece, D. J., Pisano, G., & Shuen, A. (1997). Dynamic capabilities and strategic management. *Strategic Management Journal, 18*(7), 509-533.

The Economist. (1999). The sick man of the euro. [Cited 8 August 2014.] Available from URL: http://www.economist.com/node/209559

Thomsen, S., Pedersen, T., & Kvist, H. K. (2006). Blockholder ownership: Effects on firm value in market and control based governance systems. *Journal of Corporate Finance, 12*(2), 246-269.

Tian, J. J., Haleblian, J. J., & Rajagopalan, N. (2011). The effects of board human and social capital on investor reactions to new CEO selection. *Strategic Management Journal, 32*(7), 731-747.

Tsui, A. S., Egan, T. D., & O'Reilly III, C. A. (1992). Being different: Relational demography and organizational attachment. *Administrative Science Quarterly*, 549-579.

Tsui, A. S., & O'Reilly III, C. A. (1989). Beyond simple demographic effects: The importance of relational demography in superior-subordinate dyads. *Academy of Management Journal, 32*(2), 402-423.

Tsui, A. S., Pearce, J. L., Porter, L. W., & Tripoli, A. M. (1997). Alternative approaches to the employee-organization relationship: Does investment in employees pay off? *Academy of Management Journal, 40*(5), 1089-1997.

Tuggle, C. S., Schnatterly, K., & Johnson, R. A. (2010). Attention patterns in the boardroom: How board composition and processes affect discussion of entrepreneurial issues. *Academy of Management Journal, 53*(3), 550-571.

Tuggle, C. S., Sirmon, D. G., Reutzel, C. R., & Bierman, L. (2010). Commanding board of director attention: Investigating how organizational performance and CEO duality affect board members' attention to monitoring. *Strategic Management Journal, 31*(9), 946-968.

Turban, D. B., & Greening, D. W. (1997). Corporate social performance and organizational attractiveness to prospective employees. *Academy of Management Journal, 40*(3), 658-672.

Tuschke, A., & Luber, M. (2012). Corporate governance in Germany: Converging towards shareholder value-orientation or not so much? In A. Rasheed & T. Yoshikawa (Eds.), *The convergence of corporate governance: Promise and prospects* (pp. 75-92). Hampshire, UK: Palgrave Macmillan.

Tuschke, A., Sanders, W., & Hernandez, E. (2014). Whose experience matters in the boardroom? The effects of experiential and vicarious learning on emerging market entry. *Strategic Management Journal, 35*(3), 398-418.

Tuschke, A., & Sanders, W. G. (2003). Antecedents and consequences of corporate governance reform: The case of Germany. *Strategic Management Journal, 24*(7), 631-649.

Useem, M. (1984). *The inner circle*. New York: Oxford University Press.

van Essen, M., van Oosterhout, J., & Heugens, P. P. (2013). Competition and cooperation in corporate governance: The effects of labor institutions on blockholder effectiveness in 23 European countries. *Organization Science, 24*(2), 530-551.

van Hook, J. C. (2004). *Rebuilding Germany: The creation of the social market economy, 1945–1957*. Cambridge: Cambridge University Press.

van Veen, K., & Elbertsen, J. (2008). Governance regimes and nationality diversity in corporate boards: A comparative study of Germany, the Netherlands and the United Kingdom. *Corporate Governance: An International Review, 16*(5), 386-399.

Verbeke, A., & Tung, V. (2013). The future of stakeholder management theory: A temporal perspective. *Journal of Business Ethics, 112*(3), 529-543.

von Nordenflycht, A. (2010). What is a professional service firm? Toward a theory and taxonomy of knowledge-intensive firms. *Academy of Management Review, 35*(1), 155-174.

Walls, J. L., Berrone, P., & Phan, P. H. (2012). Corporate governance and environmental performance: Is there really a link? *Strategic Management Journal, 33*(8), 885-913.

Walsh, J. P. (2005). Book review essay: Taking stock of stakeholder management. *Academy of Management Review, 30*(2), 426-438.

Webber, S. S., & Donahue, L. M. (2001). Impact of highly and less job-related diversity on work group cohesion and performance: A meta-analysis. *Journal of Management, 27*(2), 141-162.

Weber, A. (2009). An empirical analysis of the 2000 corporate tax reform in Germany: Effects on ownership and control in listed companies. *International Review of Law and Economics, 29*(1), 57-66.

Weimer, J., & Pape, J. (1999). A taxonomy of systems of corporate governance. *Corporate Governance: An International Review, 7*(2), 152-166.

Wernerfelt, B., & Montgomery, C. A. (1988). Tobin's q and the importance of focus in firm performance. *American Economic Review*, 246-250.

Werr, A., & Stjernberg, T. (2003). Exploring management consulting firms as knowledge systems. *Organization Studies, 24*(6), 881-908.

Westphal, J. D. (1999). Collaboration in the boardroom: Behavioral and performance consequences of CEO-board social ties. *Academy of Management Journal, 42*(1), 7-24.

Westphal, J. D., & Bednar, M. K. (2005). Pluralistic ignorance in corporate boards and firms' strategic persistence in response to low firm performance. *Administrative Science Quarterly, 50*(2), 262-298.

Westphal, J. D., & Fredrickson, J. W. (2001). Who directs strategic change? Director experience, the selection of new CEOs, and change in corporate strategy. *Strategic Management Journal, 22*(12), 1113-1137.

Westphal, J. D., & Milton, L. P. (2000). How experience and network ties affect the influence of demographic minorities on corporate boards. *Administrative Science Quarterly, 45*(2), 366-398.

Westphal, J. D., & Zajac, E. J. (1995). Who shall govern? CEO/board power, demographic similarity, and new director selection. *Administrative Science Quarterly, 40*(1), 60-86.

Westphal, J. D., & Zajac, E. J. (1997). Defections from the inner circle: Social exchange, reciprocity, and the diffusion of board independence in U.S. corporations. *Administrative Science Quarterly, 42*(1), 161-183.

Wiersema, M. F., & Bantel, K. A. (1992). Top management team demography and corporate strategic change. *Academy of Management Journal, 35*(1), 91-121.

Williams, K. Y., & O'Reilly, C. A. (1998). Demography and diversity in organizations: A review of 40 years of research. *Research in Organizational Behavior, 20*, 77-140.

Williamson, O. E. (1985). *The economic intstitutions of capitalism*. New York, NY: Free Press.

Windolf, P., & Beyer, J. (1996). Co-operative capitalism: Corporate networks in Germany and Britain. *British Journal of Sociology, 47*(2), 205-231.

Wooldridge, J. M. (2009). *Introductory econometrics: A modern approach* (4th ed.). Cincinnati: South-Western.

Wu, S., Levitas, E., & Priem, R. L. (2005). CEO tenure and company invention under differing levels of technological dynamism. *Academy of Management Journal, 48*(5), 859-873.

Yoshikawa, T., & Rasheed, A. A. (2009). Convergence of corporate governance: Critical review and future directions. *Corporate Governance: An International Review, 17*(3), 388-404.

Zahra, S. A., & Pearce, J. A. (1989). Boards of directors and corporate financial performance: A review and integrative model. *Journal of Management, 15*(2), 291-334.

Zajac, E. J., & Westphal, J. D. (1996). Who shall succeed? How CEO/board preferences and power affect the choice of new CEOs. *Academy of Management Journal, 39*(1), 64-90.

Zald, M. N. (1969). The power and functions of boards of directors: A theoretical synthesis. *American Journal of Sociology*, 97-111.

Zhu, D. H., & Westphal, J. D. (2014). How directors' prior experience with other demographically similar CEOs affects their appointments onto corporate boards and the consequences for CEO compensation. *Academy of Management Journal, 57*(3), 791-813.

Zona, F., Zattoni, A., & Minichilli, A. (2013). A contingency model of boards of directors and firm innovation: The moderating role of firm size. *British Journal of Management, 24*(3), 299-315.